The

Unorthodox

Life

For Ann,
With love &
blessings
Kathy

More praise for
THE UNORTHODOX LIFE

"The Unorthodox Life is an amazing book! It is mystical, practical, and inspiring. Kathy McCall has given us all a wonderful gift that will guide and illumine us as we go forward on our spiritual journey. This is the best book I have read in a long time!"

**Rev. Rosemary Fillmore-Rhea, Granddaughter of
Charles & Myrtle Fillmore, founders of the Unity
Movement, Author, *That's Just How My Spirit Travels***

"This book resonates with a gentle and congenial tone but carries a deep message. It takes the reader on a journey that is both personal and auto-biographical, one that arouses one's own story and sheds light on one's own spiritual journey. It is well told and inviting and needed as all of us today are called to see our stories as spiritual journeys, adventures that we can choose to steer into places of ever greater depth and ever more generous living."

**Matthew Fox, PhD, Theologian, Author of 30+ books, including
Original Blessing, A Spirituality Named Compassion,
and *The Coming of the Cosmic Christ***

"I wholeheartedly endorse this wise, brave, clear and profound book. Kathy McCall guides us through her vision of the revolution of the Direct Path and its transformative crucial importance at this stage of history with grace, learning, radical honesty, and humility, a humility that makes all welcome."

**Andrew Harvey, Mystic, Author, *The Direct Path, Return of the
Mother, Son of Man, The Sun at Midnight,* and *The Hope***

"As surely as inhaling of air is followed by exhaling, and night the day, so does this book follow the pattern of its creator, the Reverend Kathy McCall. McCall is a master storyteller and inherently the story gives birth to its 'point.' The Unorthodox Life: Walking Our Own Path to the Divine is filled with pragmatisms and mysticisms that lead one into a direct experience of the Divine. Nor do the points of the stories stop in the reading. As a true spiritual guide, McCall closes the chapters with exercises that encourage and assist the reader in walking the path to the Divine. This author provides inspiration in print and excites the reader with insight into the depths of his/her own psyche, with a map to navigate one's world, with understanding of self and others, and midwives an understanding of our place in the universe. This book is a keeper, a 'must read' for beginning and re-reading for advancing students of life."

Rev. Glenn Mosley, Former CEO, International Association of Unity Churches, Author, *Global Positioning for the Soul: New Thought, Ancient Wisdom*

"The Unorthodox Life is one of the most interesting and compelling accounts of an authentically evolving spiritual journey that I have read in a long time. The breadth and depth of lived spiritual experience revealed in this book is alive and growing; it is both profoundly moving and deeply instructive. If you are a person who takes science seriously, and at the same time has an inescapable feeling that rationalist materialism is not enough to make deep sense of your experience, then this is a book you owe it to yourself to read."

Jeremy Taylor, D.Min, Author, *Where People Fly and Water Runs Uphill: Using Dreams to Tap the Wisdom of the Unconscious; Dream Work: Techniques for Discovering the Creative Powers in Dreams; The Living Labyrinth: Exploring Universal Themes in Myths, Dreams, and the Symbolism of Waking Life*

THE
UNORTHODOX
LIFE

Walking Your Own
Path to the Divine

Kathy McCall

Grateful acknowledgment is made to the following for permission to reprint previously published materials:

Aurora Press Inc.: Excerpt from pages 132-133, from INITIATION, ISBN 0-943358-50-7, by Elisabeth Haich, reprinted with the permission of Aurora Press Inc. PO 573, Santa Fe, NM 87504, Copyright © 2000 Aurora Press.

HarperCollins: Excerpts from pp. xi, xii-xiii (270 words) from WE: UNDERSTANDING THE PSYCHOLOGY OF ROMANTIC LOVE by Robert A. Johnson. Copyright © 1983 by Robert A. Johnson. Reprinted by permission of HarperCollins Publishers.

Health Communications, Inc: For Jack Canfield, "The Golden Buddha" from CHICKEN SOUP FOR THE SOUL, edited by Jack Canfield and Mark Victor Hansen. Copyright © 1992 by Jack Canfield. Reprinted with the permission of Health Communications, Inc., www.hcibooks.com

Inner Traditions: For excerpts from A SPIRITUALITY NAMED COMPASSION by Matthew Fox. Copyright © 1999 by Matthew Fox. Reprinted by permission of Inner Traditions/Bear & Company, www.InnerTraditions.com

Random House, Inc: Excerpts from AFTER THE ECSTASY, THE LAUNDRY by Jack Kornfield, copyright © 2000 by Jack Kornfield. Used by permissions of Bantam Books, a division of Random House, Inc. Excerpts from THE DIRECT PATH by Andrew Harvey, copyright © 2000 by Andrew Harvey. Used by permission of Broadway Books, a division of Random House, Inc. Excerpts from MEMORIES, DREAMS AND REFLECTIONS by C.G. Jung, edited by Aniela Jaffe, translated by Richard & Clara Winston, translation copyright © 1961, 1962, 1963 and renewed 1989, 1990, 1991 by Random House, Inc. Used by permission of Pantheon Books, a division of Random House, Inc.

ISBN 978-0-9841140-0-9

Interior and cover design by DreamWriter (dreamwriterservices.com)

River Sanctuary Publishing
PO Box 1561
Felton, CA 95018
www.RiverSanctuaryPublishing.com
Dedicated to the spiritual awakening of the New Earth

For Chris and Justin
with love always

Thank you to all those who
have supported my journey and
this creative effort!

CONTENTS

INTRODUCTION

Grandfather, Great Spirit,...You have set the powers of the four quarters of the earth to cross each other. You have made me cross the good road, and the road of difficulties, and where they cross, the place is holy. Day in, day out, forevermore, you are the life of things.

Black Elk, Oglala Sioux[1]

This is not just another spiritual book. It is written at a time of great menace and danger in the world in order to help you awaken and reconcile the powers within and without. It describes four stages of the spiritual path in ways that are easily accessible whether you are a beginning or advanced seeker. Personal stories, examples, and practical methods are presented so that you can give birth to a more enlightened consciousness and a new world.

I have been willing to open my own life to express what I have learned and to share some of my very personal experiences, specifically related to my spiritual path. My journey has included an exploration of Eastern studies, Astrology, the Western Mystical Tradition, Creation Spirituality, Jungian thought,

Dream Work, and Shamanism. Along the way I embraced the teachings of Unity, one of the New Thought traditions with roots in Transcendentalism and a special niche in the world as a more progressive and mystical Christianity, and I became a Unity Minister. My eclectic path unfolds in the following pages through the various encounters and anecdotes. Some of the stories may be familiar, but they are brought together for readers to experience in a new original context.

Walking my own path to the Divine has been an initiation into my power. It is a path that calls each one of us to our destiny for it is the spiritual journey that we all take, even in spite of ourselves. It is essential at this time that we consciously understand the path to enlightenment for the sake of our species and our Earth. We have the power to give birth to a universal humanity that is awake to its oneness. It is our calling and responsibility, and each of us must walk our own path of awakening.

I have been aware of my spiritual path for most of my life; however, it took years to discover a framework that would help me to see its universal dimensions. This discovery has been an evolving process that I actively engaged when leading groups on transformational journeys in my ministry over a period of weeks and sometimes months. In facilitating the spiritual quest for others I discovered my own inner depths as well. I also found that the path to the Divine can be named in four stages since four is the foundation number of wholeness and completion. Throughout all of creation many examples of four can be seen:

There are four faces, or four ages: the face of the child, the face of the adolescent, the face of the adult, the face of the aged.

There are four directions or four winds, four seasons, and four quarters of the universe, four races of man and woman—red, yellow, black, and white.

There are four things that breathe: those that crawl, those that fly, those that are two-legged, those that are four-legged.

There are four things above the earth: sun, moon, stars, planets.

There are four parts to the green things: roots, stem, leaves, fruit.

There are four divisions of time: day, night, moon, year.

There are four elements: fire, water, air, earth.

Even the human heart is divided into four compartments....[2]

Having explored the number four for many years in various spiritual frameworks, it was exciting to meet others along the path who had delved into the power of four on their own mystical journeys, especially Matthew Fox, Jeremy Taylor, and also Andrew Harvey. Matthew and Jeremy have been important teachers in my life, and I was so blessed to study with them at the former University of Creation Spirituality, founded by Matthew Fox. There I learned the four paths of that tradition: The *Via Positiva, Via Negativa, Via Creativa,* and

Via Transformativa. My experience of those paths had a tremendous impact on my work and continues to enrich my approach to ministry.

I was also delighted to discover Andrew Harvey's book *The Direct Path* since it confirmed my conclusions about the Divine potential in each one of us without the need for gurus or outside authorities, and it presented a framework that I have also found to be very powerful and that I have chosen to use in this book, with his permission. This four-fold map that can guide us in our personal and collective heart awakening is a metaphor for our own relationship with the Divine. It explains the path that we walk whether we are conscious of it or not. The four stages are: FALLING IN LOVE, ENGAGEMENT, SACRED MARRIAGE, and BIRTHING.

Though we generally think of falling in love and getting married in regard to a person who is our true love, this map describes the relationship with our true Self, with God and all of creation as we begin seeing with our heart. My use of this particular framework is to provide one interpretation of this universal archetypal Path based on my own experience.

During a Fall Program that I created in my former ministry at Unity Temple of Santa Cruz, the congregation and I journeyed together in Sunday Services and supportive study groups. Through meditation, discussion and spiritual practice, we activated the power of the archetypal path to the Divine. This can be done individually and in any group setting where the goal is greater spiritual enlightenment through practice and action. Becoming both "mystics" and "prophets" is an important result, for the nature of the path is such that one cannot remain complacent. A mystic is one who sees, while a prophet is one who acts, thus "interfering with injustice," in the words of Matthew Fox.[3]

This book presents the four stages of the path, each containing: 1) a description of the Stage of the Path; 2) an autobiographical account of the important spiritual events of my life as experienced in that Stage; 3) three chapters with deeper insights, explanations and stories of the Stage; and 4) Spiritual Practice exercises at the end of each of these chapters.

It is my prayer for you as you read this book that you discover your own unique path to the Divine that you have been walking your entire life, and that you awaken your personal power. I invite you to commit to spiritual practice by completing the exercises at the end of each chapter. These include: prayer, meditation, physical activity, and journaling. Keep a journal as you read and practice, noting your thoughts and your dreams. This will enable you to find your own connections and help the ideas become more real to you. I suggest that you set an intention to journey through these four paths in a deep personal effort to wake up, to discover the power of love, and to become consciously involved in co-creating a new world.

Stage One
FALLING IN LOVE
—From Complacency to Passion—

Experience

An awareness of Divine Presence

A honeymoon

Seeing the Divine Light in everything

Challenge

Purification of the senses

Danger

Fear and bewilderment

Process

Exposing ego's games to the light of
    Divine Awareness

Inner analysis

Facing past trauma and its effects

Practice

Devotion to prayer, meditation, study

Cultivation of compassion and loving kindness

The first part of this wonderful stage of falling in love with the Divine is what is called in many mystical traditions the honeymoon stage. The seeker is amazed and entranced by what he or she is discovering within his or her depths; the visions and experiences are welcomed with rapture.

What then happens, however, is that this honeymoon period evolves into a period of self-purification in which the seeker strives passionately to make her being ever clearer and ever more open to the Divine. This first great purification on the Path is known in many mystical systems as the purification of the senses, where we prepare to hold more of the Divine... It entails inner analysis, and an exposing of the ego's games by facing our issues and the self-betrayals that society conditions us to. We do that by increasing the light of Divine awareness through spiritual practice, prayer, meditation, service, and greater devotion to the Divine.

Andrew Harvey, *The Direct Path*, 52

Chapter 1

FALLING IN LOVE

$\mathcal{H}$ow does one know the pivotal experiences that are the signposts of a spiritual journey? It requires deep reflection and meditation and the power of story itself to reveal our path to the Divine. My story is filled with mystical experiences, but the ones that need to be told are those that were the key events in my own unique Path. They unfold in a natural order within the four-fold framework to follow. This biographical account can be found continuing at the beginning of each section. May these experiences serve as a map and a guiding light to others!

My mother was my spiritual teacher. She was bi-polar and was misdiagnosed for 30 years, thought to be paranoid schizophrenic. She was given incorrect medication and literally hundreds of shock treatments. Every time they occurred she would return home from the hospital having forgotten my name.

Between her highs and lows—those months when she was rational, she was a very conscious being, an amazingly wise sage, in fact. Her suffering and her incredible awareness was a paradox that caused me to ask the question, "why" in my childhood and throughout my life. My own pain from the experience catapulted me onto my spiritual journey at a young age. I longed to find God and I learned firsthand about the insanity that can come when one does not have the proper container for the powerful numinous energies of the psyche.

My mother spent at least one to two months in the hospital every year of my childhood. I became her rescuer as a young adult, often bringing her home on hospital passes and trying to talk her back into "reality." The day that I could read her mind and anticipate what she was going to say when she was in another world altogether was the day that I realized the danger of being pulled into her realm. The awareness has served as a powerful protection in my life.

When I was a teenager I had a lesson from her that I have never forgotten. One day she came to me and said, "Kathy, we are going to take a gold trip, follow me." She put gold slippers on her feet, and then led me to our large bookshelf where after pausing briefly, she pulled out a gold book, opened it up, and pointing to a word, she read, "Faith." Turning to me she said, "This will be a faith journey." Then we walked through the house, as she picked up different gold objects, relating each one to faith until we had taken a long full circle journey back to the bookcase. These simple quests were repeated from time to time with different themes. This strange magic began my education about the power of symbols, journey, and the importance of connections. It was an unusual foreshadowing of my later work as a minister, synthesizing truth from various teachings, and leading people on transformational journeys, helping them to see the connections between the spiritual path and daily life.

During my teenage years, in Salt Lake City, where I was raised, I would attend open AA meetings with my mother, after she joined Alcoholics Anonymous. My parents were both alcoholics, and fortunately my mother was able to find help through that program. From those meetings I learned about the power of storytelling and spiritual practice.

I always loved my mother's company because we would have wonderful conversations. She would read to me from *Science of Mind* magazine, while I sat across from her in the living room overlooking the Wasatch Range of the Rocky Mountains. It was there my early interest in metaphysics was fueled. She told me the family stories and shared about her own spiritual path.

Her call to the journey began when she was the first person in her family to leave the Mormon Church. She was the granddaughter of Joseph F. Smith, the sixth president of the Church (like the Pope in the Catholic faith), so it was quite scandalous. She married my father, who was a Mason, promising her parents that she would convert him. Instead, she became the black sheep, studied metaphysics and Astrology, and began to develop her psychic powers. I inherited her gift for Astrology and have practiced it professionally for many years. I was never raised Mormon, but growing up in that environment as an "outsider" planted the seeds of religious rebellion.

My father was very private about his spirituality. He was not religious, but became a Grand Master of his Masonic Lodge, so I believe that he must have been more versed in the mysteries than I ever realized. The Lodge seemed to be a social organization that helped him to form friendships and connections important to his architectural hardware business. He furnished hardware on many large buildings including several Mormon Temples, as well as the original MGM Hotel in Las Vegas. Perhaps he was a successful self-made businessman because of his aware-ness of greater principles. He provided for his family responsibly despite his disease of alcoholism and supported my mother through years of her mental illness.

My father had a spiritual side as well, though we seldom discussed it. I have a particularly vivid memory of his belief in God, whom he referred to as "The Man Upstairs" or "The Great Architect of the Universe." My mother had been taken off to the hospital once again and my dad and I were left at home both feeling very sad and helpless. The first morning after she left, my father created a spontaneous ritual that has stayed with me ever since. He woke me out of sleep and told me to put my robe and slippers on. Then he led the way with a flashlight through the early morning darkness. We came to a flowering bush at the side of the house and there knelt down on the earth. He asked me to watch in silence as he dug a small hole in the dirt. Then he produced a piece of paper on which he had written the word "gloom." We proceeded to bury gloom. He covered the grave with dirt and then pulled a toothpick cross out of his pocket. He asked me to place it on the site. He then gave a little eulogy in which we together released gloom from our lives and thanked God for our blessings. The ceremony ended just as the sun was rising. That scene has forever remained etched in my memory as a symbol of the power we each have to cast off the negative and invoke new life. "Weeping may endure for a night but joy comes in the morning."

After a sudden illness, my father rallied from his death-bed and lived for an additional year, during which time he sold his business in order to provide for my mother after his death. She lived eighteen more years without having to work a single day. Dad taught me the importance of commitment and responsibility, and his generosity was an early lesson in the power of prosperity.

Strong parental influence was true for my brother and sister as well, though we all experienced it differently. I was the youngest of three children. I am fifteen years younger than my brother, Keith, and nine years younger than my sister, Cheryl. Because I was still very young when they left home, we developed our relationships more as adults. Keith was employed by my father for many years in the hardware business, and has created his own companies since. He returned to furnish the hardware and doors on the second MGM Hotel in Las Vegas, and that created the opportunity for many other hotel building projects there. My sister and I call him the man with the "Midas Touch," since everything he undertakes is financially successful.

My brother has eight children and thirty two grandchildren. He has been an example to me of commitment to family even in the midst of incredible challenges in life.

Cheryl and I share spiritual values. We have a unique and complex relationship as sisters, having explored some of the mystical arena together and having the luxury of sharing dreams and deep personal experiences. I lived with her for a brief period of transition in my life while we both attended the same graduate program. Though she has had a varied career path, she seems to have found her passion as a healer.

She has been both sister and friend and her two children and five grandchildren have always felt like my own immediate family. Cheryl has been very supportive, and from her I have learned the power of a compassionate heart.

My spiritual education at home led me to explore Eastern religions in the search for a guru. Frustrated after three years of college, I turned to Alan Watts and Paramahansa Yogananda and fell in love with the man Jesus whom I had discovered in the red-letter edition of my Dad's Masonic Bible. I left my parents' home, dropped out of school, and made my way to San Francisco as a flower child in the late 60's where I led a dual life working in the financial district on weekdays and donning my "hippie" persona for the rest of the week. These were the days of peace protests and sit-ins at Golden Gate Park, as I awakened to my own sense of rebellion against the war, the government, and all that seemed to be false in our society at the time.

This period was followed by a pilgrimage to Mexico where I discovered meditation and gave up the use of all "unnatural substances," partly from sheer terror of eternal residence in a Mexican jail, but mostly because something deeper than fear was calling to me.

A friend and I traveled to San Miguel de Allende, five hours north of Mexico City, where we stayed for six weeks studying Spanish, Art, and Writing at an English-speaking school. We immersed ourselves in the culture, and then traveled throughout Mexico on buses and trains.

I plunged into a timeless state while staying in a small village north of Acapulco. We had gathered several friends along the way, and we each slept in a hammock under a thatched roof without walls. There were no watches or clocks and we would awaken with the sun and bathe in the lagoon across the road. My diet consisted of fruit sold by a woman on the beach or fresh fish cooked in the native huts every evening. The weeks were an endless meditation with dolphins swimming in translucent waves by daylight, and stars falling from an infinite universe each night. It was a cosmic experience that left me awestruck and overcome with a profound longing for God.

This period of leaving home and falling in love with life and the grand adventure of the journey was preparation for deeper engagement of the spiritual path. I was a complete innocent, about to walk into the temptations that always occur after initial awakening.

Chapter 2

FALLING INTO LOVE

The initial awakening occurs because we have forgotten our Divinity. There is a Jewish legend that all souls existed with God before the creation of the universe, carefully stored beneath the Divine throne until the time of birth. When a child is conceived, God removes the soul from the Divine realm and plants it in the mother's womb. On the journey to earth, an angel accompanies the soul and during its gestation instructs it in all the mysteries of the universe. At the time the baby is born, however, the angel taps it lightly and it promptly forgets everything it has learned. Therefore it bursts into tears. In the Greek tradition it was believed that we drink of the waters of Lethe, a spring near the entrance of the underworld, which blots out memory of the past and allows us to enter earth life with a clean slate. We are writing our book of destiny and we must let go of the detailed memory of other lives in order to write the chapter of this life experience. Lifetimes may be required before we are wise enough to enter without drinking Lethe's waters.

The other spring near the underworld entrance is that of Mnemosyne or memory:

> Thou shalt find to the left of the House of Hades a Well-spring
>
> And by the side thereof standing a white cypress.
>
> To this Well-spring approach not near.
>
> But thou shalt find another by the Lake of Memory,
>
> Cold water flowing forth, and there are Guardians before it.
>
> Say: "I am a child of Earth and of Starry Heaven;
>
> But my race is of Heaven (alone). This ye know yourselves.
>
> And lo, I am parched with thirst and I perish. Give me quickly
>
> The cold water flowing forth from the Lake of Memory."
>
> And of themselves they will give thee to drink from the holy Well-spring,
>
> And thereafter among the other Heroes thou shalt have lordship...[1]

Stories throughout time speak to the truth that we do have access to all of the mysteries of the universe. Each of us has the capacity to become enlightened—to find personal Divinity, to discover the Christ, the Spirit of Divine Love within us. And we must take our journeys to wake up and remember the truth.

Finding personal Divinity means "falling into love" with life, with ourselves, with God, and with all of creation. It is becoming awestruck with the wonders of the universe.

This is the place in our journey where we move from complacency to passion.

And we do that by seeing with the heart. Think about a moment when you have felt madly in love, when everything takes on a special glow. The poet Rumi said, "All your talk is worthless when compared to one whisper of the Beloved."[2]

When we are in that state of love we are seeing with the heart and we can feel this about any aspect of life—the whisper of a leaf, a bird, a child. We are not generally focused on seeing with the heart, however, since we have forgotten. We are conditioned by the outer world—in a consensus trance.

Sometimes though, we have those moments of mystical epiphany when our perception shifts and we see the world with new eyes. This happened for me quite dramatically when I was at the top of Mt. Tamalpais, just north of San Francisco, with my sister Cheryl and some friends. I was twenty-one and we were celebrating the occasion. We spent the day exploring the beauty of nature inspired by the radiant blue Pacific below us on one side to the west and the city of San Francisco, in miniature, off to the southeast.

I stood listening to the wind rustling through the trees and the sound of the leaves on the bushes enveloping me like delicate chimes. At that moment I suddenly became one with the wind, the trees, the sky, and the earth. My sister and her friends were no longer separate from me, but we were all expressions of One Mind. Suddenly every person and every being in the entire world—in all of creation were part of this magnificent whole. I was no longer separate from God. I was united with everything. This state of total bliss lasted for several hours and completely altered my view of the world. It was a sacred experience that informs me of our oneness to this day.

It is possible to see with the heart even without the mystical breakthrough. When we have forgotten, it takes pausing and "practicing the Presence of God" by consciously looking for the good or the beauty in a place, a person, or an experience. Rumi said, "You'll be forgiven for forgetting that what you really want is love's confusing joy."[3]

It is love's joy that we gain by taking a conscious journey into the heart of the Divine. Let us walk our own Path with full awareness in order to:

- *Remember our Divinity*
- *See with our heart*
- *Find inner peace amidst the outer changes in the world*
- *Support ourselves and others in spiritual practice*
- *Make a difference in the world by making a difference in our own lives*
- *Become both mystic and prophet*

It is essential that we overcome complacency and awaken from our consensus trance for the good of all beings in our world today. There are those moments when we do see—when we realize our love and oneness through a mystical experience, a brush with our own death, or through years of discipline and study and then a sudden breakthrough when everything is illumined. On this journey into the depths of love the main requirement is that as heroes or heroines in our own life stories, we attempt to see with the heart.

Children are masters of the heart and can always tell us about love. An eight year old boy named Dave said, "Love will find you, even if you are trying to hide from it. I been trying to hide from it since I was five, but the girls keep finding me."[4]

Love will always find us! It is all-inclusive, embracing our wholeness, both the dark and the light. It is reflected in the marriage vow when we say "I take you in health and in sickness, in wealth and in poverty." True love embraces all of us.

In this first station of falling in love, we begin with a romantic honeymoon where everything is wonderful. We have seen with the heart, and then suddenly we discover that we have come face to face with the shadow—those unconscious parts of ourselves that we avoid. It is now time to integrate them through a process of release and self-purification.

This is precisely what I experienced after leaving home, going to San Francisco, having my mystical awakening on Mt. Tamalpais, then going off to Mexico and falling in love with life. I felt invincible—everything was possible, even enlightenment. It was a perfect preparation for the test to follow. It was time for my ego to be purified. This happens in different ways for each of us.

Buddhist Jack Kornfield tells a Swedish story that I love which speaks to this honeymoon experience of self-purification:

> Because of the mishaps of her parents, a young princess named Aris must be betrothed to a fearful dragon. When the king and queen tell her, she becomes frightened for her life. But recovering her wits, she goes out beyond the market to seek a wise woman, who has raised twelve children and twenty nine grandchildren, and knows the ways of dragons and men.
>
> The wise woman tells Aris that she indeed must marry the dragon, but that there are proper ways to approach him. She then gives instructions for the wedding night. In particular, the princess is bidden to wear ten beautiful gowns, one on top of another.
>
> The wedding takes place. A feast is held in the palace, after which the dragon carries the princess off to his bed-chamber. When the dragon advances toward his bride, she stops him, saying that she must carefully remove her wedding attire before offering her heart to him. And he too, she adds (instructed by the wise woman), must properly remove his attire. To this he willingly agrees.
>
> "As I take off each layer of my gown, you must also remove a layer." Then, taking off the first gown, the princess watches as the dragon sheds his outer layer of

scaly armor. Though it is painful, the dragon has done this periodically before. But then the princess removes another gown, and then another. Each time the dragon finds he too must claw off a deeper layer of scales. By the fifth gown the dragon begins to weep copious tears at the pain. Yet the princess continues.

With each successive layer the skin becomes more tender and his form softens. He becomes lighter and lighter. When the princess removes her tenth gown, the dragon releases the last vestige of dragon form and emerges as a man, a fine prince whose eyes sparkle like a child's, released at last from the ancient spell of his dragon form. Princess Aris and her new husband are then left to the pleasures of their bridal chamber, to fulfill the last advice of the wise woman with twelve children and twenty-nine grandchildren.[5]

As in a dream, all the figures in such a story can be found within us—the dragon, the attending princess, the wise grandmother, the irresponsible king and queen, the hidden prince, and the unknown one who cast the enchantment long ago.[6]

The story reveals that the journey of falling into love is not about going right into the light. It is not about falling into love and living happily ever after from that moment.

Receiving grace, opening to illumination, becoming wise and knowing Divine Love has not always been easy, even for the masters. It includes a cleansing and deep purification and can be very difficult to cast off our own scales—our own armor. "Fortunately, as the dragon skins are removed it is not all pain. There comes a lightness as each wedding gown is removed, as if angels are bringing blessings as well."[7]

If you have ever been in love you know this experience. You go into the initial high where you see the world with new eyes. You have on the "rose-colored glasses" and the world is a beautiful place to be. And then you discover the tragic flaw.

This other person is not as perfect as you had hoped. This container of your love has a crack. He or she has a few defects that are very disappointing. And not only that, but your old wounds and behaviors are emerging—somehow you thought with this other person, maybe it would be different. It is a strange logic that causes one to believe that it will be different because the gods are smiling on you this time, for yours is the only love in the whole world.

When the flaws arise, we have to persevere, remove the scales, the armor, from our own heart and from our own bodies—where we store our tension. We learn how to step from these old skins so that we may see and act from an open heart.

There is an old Sufi tale where Nasruddin and his friend were sitting in a café drinking tea and talking about life and love.

"How come you never got married, Nasruddin?" asked his friend.

"Well," said Nasruddin, "To tell you the truth, I spent

my youth looking for the perfect woman. In Cairo, I met a beautiful and intelligent woman, with eyes like dark olives, but she was unkind. Then in Baghdad, I met a woman who was a wonderful and generous soul, but we had no interests in common. One woman after another would seem just right, but there would always be something missing. Then one day, I met her. She was beautiful, intelligent, generous, kind. We had everything in common. In fact, she was perfect."

"Well," said Nasruddin's friend, "What happened? Why didn't you marry her?"

Nasruddin sipped his tea reflectively. "Well," he replied, "It's a sad thing, seems she was looking for the perfect man."[8]

The Path is not about finding perfection in our self or others or even life. It is about falling into love with *what is*—seeing with the heart, and then everything is transformed.

The longing for love and the movement of love is underneath all that we do. The happiness we find in life is the discovery of this capacity to love, to have a loving, free, and wise relationship with all of life.

We are all welcomed and loved by God—by all of creation, and God has been waiting for us to take off our scales and awaken to Divine Love.

So pack your bags, open your map, and get ready to go exploring. Find the prize of your personal Divinity by falling into love with yourself, with God, with others, and with all of creation.

As you do, just watch—you will discover angels all around instructing you in the mysteries of the universe.

SPIRITUAL PRACTICE

Falling Into Love

Prayer

Invoke the Presence and Power of God and ask to know more of Divine Love. Affirm throughout each day, "*I am one with Divine Love.*"

Meditation

Sit quietly in silence and relax your mind and body. Take time to create an inner feeling of being loved and loving, while breathing deeply. Send this loving feeling out into the world.

Physical Activity

Take a walk in nature. Fall in love with different aspects of creation—a flower, a tree, an animal, a person...

Journaling

Describe your experiences in meditation and on your walk. Write an intention for the study of this book. What would you like to achieve?

Chapter 3

FALLING INTO PASSION

Maurice Sendak, author of the wonderful children's book *Where The Wild Things Are,* once recounted that he sent to a young reader a card with a picture of a wild thing on it, and the boy's mother wrote back that her son loved the card so much he ate it. He didn't seem to care that it was an original Maurice Sendak drawing. He just saw it, he loved it, he ate it...Passion is a state of love and hunger. It is also a state of enthusiasm, which means to be possessed by a God or a Goddess, by a wild thing.[1]

*W*hen most of us think of the honeymoon experience passion is a word that comes to mind. Passion is a doorway into the Divine because it awakens our ability to see with the heart.

The princess who was betrothed to a dragon tricked him—telling him that she could not give her heart until he removed his scales. (J.R.R. Tolkien once said, "It does not do to leave a live dragon out of your calculations if you live near him.")[2] And though it was painful, he clawed away his armor until he finally emerged from his dragon form as a prince. As we let go of our dragon scales, our fears, our false beliefs, our wounds, we remove the armor from our heart so that we can see with eyes of love and experience true passion. Seeing with the heart is the way to invoke our Divine awareness.

Passionate love is a metaphor for our relationship with the Divine. We must learn to harness and channel that passion for our own spiritual awakening and for the good of all. The true nature of passion is the longing for God and often we look for God in our romantic relationships. It has been said that passionate love is a possession, a kind of Divine madness. We have heard stories about being struck by Cupid's arrow, causing us to fall in love with the first person our eyes behold. And though it sounds frightening, we often leave our childhoods and set off on the heroic adventure in search of that magical, mystical encounter—that enchanted evening when our eyes lock across a crowded room and we find our beloved.

According to Robert Johnson, "Romantic love is the single greatest energy system in the Western psyche. In our culture it has supplanted religion as the arena in which men and women seek meaning, transcendence, wholeness, and ecstasy."[3]

Romantic love is also unique to the West. In Eastern

cultures, we find that married couples love each other with great warmth, often with a great stability and devotion. But their love is not romantic love, and does not impose the impossible demands and expectations that love in our culture does.

Robert Johnson continues:

> For romantic love does not just mean loving someone; it means being "in love." ...We believe we have found the ultimate meaning of life, revealed in another human being. We feel we are finally completed, that we have found the missing parts of ourselves. Life suddenly seems to have wholeness...an intensity that lifts us high above the ordinary plane of existence. For us, these are too often the sure signs of "true love." The psychological package includes an unconscious demand that our lover or spouse always provide us with this feeling of ecstasy, passion, and intensity.
>
> ...Despite our ecstasy when we are "in love," much of our time may be spent with a deep sense of loneliness, alienation, and frustration over an inability to make genuinely loving and committed relationships. Often we may feel it is the other person's fault, ignoring the unconscious expectations and demands we impose on our relationships and other people.
>
> This is the great wound in the Western psyche.... Carl Jung said that if you find the psychic wound in an individual or people, there you also find their path to consciousness.

...The ideal of romantic love burst into Western society during the middle ages. It first appeared in our litera-ture in the myth of Tristan and Iseult, then in the love songs of the troubadours. It was called "Courtly Love"; its model was the brave knight who worshipped a fair lady as his inspiration, the symbol of all beauty and per-fection, the ideal that moved him to be noble, spiritual, refined, and high-minded.[4]

In the story of Tristan and Iseult, a love potion is taken and they fall in love mistakenly and end up in a three year enchantment. Have you ever fallen in love with the wrong person? Have you been in a temporary enchantment? I suppose that my "rose-colored glasses" are not unique. Even the love affairs that ultimately come to an end serve the purpose of introducing us to passion.

Actually, as I was writing this section of the book I realized that it was my parents' wedding anniversary. They were married forty-five years when my father died. This would have been their 70th wedding anniversary.

They had an exciting, passionate meeting. My mother, Rhoda, was invited to go on a blind date. She had a boyfriend overseas so she did not date, but she agreed to accompany her friend Jane on a double date only if the other man was tall. She was very tall herself and quite self-conscious about it. When Jane arrived at her house with the two men, the date turned out to be short so they traded dates. Thus my mother ended up with my dad whose name was Ralph, and they all went to the Old Mill, a very romantic dinner and dancing restaurant in Salt Lake City.

My mother was won over by his humor. He was already quite bald in his 20's, and almost the first thing he said to her was, "I'll have you know that I am not losing my hair. It falls out and I throw it away."

They danced and took a walk by the stream, and my father proposed on the first night. Mom was engaged to a Mormon missionary who was overseas, but her response to my dad was "maybe." I have often felt very grateful that the relationship with the missionary did not work out!

When my dad took her home from the date that night, my mother's father, upset that she was out late, stepped out onto the porch just as Dad was trying to kiss her, and yelled, "Rhoda, get in here!" My dad jumped over the banister and ran away, and she thought that she would never see him again. But he returned the next day with flowers, and a year later, a wedding ring. She left the Mormon Church and wore a red wedding dress when she married him because he loved her in red. It was wonderfully scandalous.

My parents' meeting reminds me of a story told about a little girl named Lottie, aged 9 who was asked, "How did your mom and dad meet?" She said, "They were at a dance party at a friend's house. Then they went for a drive, but their car broke down…It was a good thing because it gave them a chance to find out about their values."[5]

In our time, we have mixed Courtly Love into our relationships as a value, but we still hold the medieval belief that true love has to be the ecstatic adoration of a person who carries for us the image of perfection. It is said that love is blind, and may well be. And yet on the other hand, there is something most amazing about it for it allows us to see the true angelic nature of another person—the Divinity within. Passion awakens our ability to see with the heart and is a doorway into the Divine.

We may wake up one day and wonder what we saw in a person—and it may have been all projection. But it hopefully allowed us to remove our own scales and armor and to experience the power of passion.

Actress and Singer Cher once said, "A girl can wait for the right man to come along, but in the meantime that still doesn't mean she can't have a wonderful time with all the wrong ones." And Mae West said, "To err is human, but it feels divine." Even in our errors and illusions we catch a glimpse of the Divine that lives in us. What we see in another is a reflection of the numinous.

The true nature of passion is the ultimate longing for God, so as we follow our passion, we find God. We may wonder how this can be when we keep running into trouble rather than God?

My parents stayed married, and it was not an easy road; however, they had a bond of love that transcended the loss of romantic love and kept them together for years. There was an underlying passion which was tempered through the years of history. But even when it does not work out for us, we have had our hearts opened—we have felt passion, and the sense of being fully alive. As Shakespeare said, "Tis better to have loved and lost, than never to have loved at all."

Whether we are in relationship or single, our passion for the Divine is important to cultivate. Passion is power. It is what we are most deeply curious about, most hungry for, will not want to lose in life. It is whatever we pursue merely for its own sake, what we study when there are no tests to take, what we create though no one may ever see it. It makes us lose all sense of time. It is what we would do if we were not worried about consequences, money, or time.[6]

Charles Fillmore, co-founder of Unity, equated it with zeal. He said, "It is the affirmative impulse of existence; its command is *Go forward!*"[7] In our relationships, in our journeys, in all of our pursuits, it is what burns like a smoldering ember beneath everything.

Teilhard de Chardin said, "Someday, after we have mastered the winds, the waves, the tides and gravity, we shall harness for God the energies of love. Then for the second time in the history of the world, we will have discovered fire."[8]

Passion is always there for me in the spiritual work of ministry. I may not always feel it, but at times a simple experience invokes it and I know it is there as intensely as it ever was—the burning of my heart's desire to know God and to awaken that longing in others. I think my entire life has been about the search for God, the search for love.

In the early days I had a journal that I kept for years. It began in high school and I would write about whomever I was dating and the details of our conversation. "Tonight Ronnie kissed me and I told him that 'first base' was as far as he was going." Then it evolved through the ensuing years. The journal was strictly reserved for love relationships, and it always included a deep longing. At some point the longing changed and the tone became more spiritual, "Dear God, when will I know more of your presence in my life? Oh God, let me experience the Divine flame of your love!"

When we ignore our passions, we dam up our energies and cut ourselves off from them. When we do not demonstrate our passions in the world, they will demonstrate themselves to us as needs, and if those needs are not met, they become symptoms of one sort or another.

"Summoned or not, the God will come," reads the inscription carved over the stone door of psychologist Carl Jung's house.

> So if we are determined to be lovers, we shall have to accept and acknowledge our passions. And then of course we rise being led into mysterious, uncharted, hazardous places, but we can be assured that our lives will never be dull.[9]

It is the Divine saying, "I am a fire—jump in, burn, be transfigured and give the whole of your life away for me by following your heart—following your love—wherever it may take you." And what have we got to lose, except our illusions?

How then do we become empowered with a vision that sees God burning in everything?

> Body, heart, mind, and soul have to be in the continual earthquake of longing....Let us see this world through the eyes of Christ. Let us see this world through the eyes of Buddha—Let us see this world through the eyes of Rumi—with all beings blazing in the Divine light. Not an illusion but filled with the living presence....Let us see this world as beings who are willing to risk their whole lives because we are awake to the beauty, the glory, the majesty, the wonder, the preciousness of life.[10]

We see with eyes of love and we awaken to the pain and to the joy of the world—and from that we are filled with a deep passion to change the world. For then passion becomes compassion.

What about when we simply do not feel passion? There are times of stagnation or depression. When we have lost our inner passion it is complacency that must be overcome. Even the most ardent lovers tend to be placated and lulled by love. Comfortable, we may take our relationships for granted, and a great complacency descends. This can be a precarious time for love.

We see it in our own lives in small ways as we cope with day to day responsibilities, just trying to deal with stress. We have seen it in our country, in our world. Symptoms of a developing problem can include a dull acceptance of everything, the desire to remain safe by traveling only familiar paths, and an indefinable feeling that something is missing. The cure for this complacency involves a willingness to step a little more boldly into paths that excite and astound and renew.

Dull routines have a way of insidiously creeping into our lives: Sunday morning breakfast after church at the same restaurant; Wednesdays with in-laws; Fridays at the movies, going to work the same way, doing the same thing day after day, week after week. What is so needed in such situations is a serendipitous act, a surprise dinner, an unexpected gift, a little craziness to shake up this deadly, habitual existence. Love's very essence is surprise and amazement. To make love a prisoner of the mundane is to take away its passion and lose it forever.

Rumi said,

> Passion makes the old medicine new:
>
> Passion lops off the bough of weariness.
>
> Passion is the elixir that renews:
>
> How can there be weariness
>
> When passion is present?
>
> Oh, don't sigh heavily from fatigue:
>
> Seek passion, seek passion, seek passion![11]

Falling Into Passion

Prayer

Invoke the Presence and Power of God and ask for greater passion. Affirm passionately: *"Divine Love now expresses through me as passion and enthusiasm."*

Meditation

Sit quietly in silence and relax your mind and body. Imagine yourself bathed in the fire of the heart, filled with the love of God. Then send that love out to all living beings.

Physical Activity

Play some powerful music that you love, and dance to it; abandon yourself to passion. Let yourself go until you feel ecstatic.

Journaling

Write about your experiences in meditation and dance. List some of your passions and their need for expression.

Chapter 4

FALLING INTO GOD

*W*ho is this God we are falling in love with and feeling so passionate about anyway? Sometimes no matter what we do it feels like God is hiding from us. Some Eastern traditions speak of God as playing hide and seek—that God is within every aspect of creation, but that once we enter the earth plane, we forget.

The Sufi mystics say that our essential self, God, is hidden from us by "a hundred thousand veils of illusion," and that we must take a journey to wake up and free ourselves from "maya," or illusion.

I prefer the idea that our purpose is not to escape the great "illusion," but to divinize ourselves and all of life. Each of us is the Christ in potential. "Christ," in this context means the perfect pattern of wholeness in all of creation. We are here to unfold and blossom into this realized being that we are destined to awaken. We take our journeys to become instruments of love, sacred passion, and power for the transformation and regeneration of all. And we discover that our personal Divinity was there all the time and the best way to find it is through surrender—what we might call "falling into God."

Why was the idea of *falling* used to describe being in love? It evokes the image of the Fool Card in the tarot deck where the fool is stepping off the cliff, while looking up and smiling innocently. Falling in love involves a similar leap while remaining oblivious to the question of whether or not there is a net to catch us.

What is the nature of falling?

- *Falling takes us by surprise.*
- *It often involves surrender.*
- *We may get hurt.*
- *We may feel protected.*
- *We may feel both hurt and protected.*

When I was involved in a prior relationship, I was in the process of moving, and I fell down a flight of stairs. It took me by surprise, caught me off guard. I injured the *piras forma* muscle in my hip, which tightened the t-band in my leg, and I spent the first three months of this committed relationship in physical therapy. It seemed to be a very bad omen, and I still have a wounded hip—like Jacob. But I did come out of it all with a new consciousness, much like Jacob wrestling with the angel and having his name changed from Jacob to Israel.

In retrospect, it was a fall into unconsciousness first. The old fool, the trickster God, will take us places we might never go willingly so we can grow up and awaken. Even when things do not succeed, they really do, because our hearts get broken open, or we grow a little closer to knowing God and to realizing our own Divinity.

Falling may be a surprise when we take the risk, step off the cliff, and the net does catch us because we fall into the arms of the Divine. God is often described as having comforting arms, and though God is not anthro-pomorphic, we must use metaphors for God.

God has been described as Father, as masculine energy, as protector, as a Powerful Fire, a Great Wind, a Holy Spirit, the Breath of Life, a Mighty King, Great Creator, Sovereign Majesty, Jehovah, Elohim, Omni-presence, Omnipotence, Omniscience.

God has been described as Mother, as a Soaring Mother Eagle, a Gathering Mother Hen, a Midwife, a ferocious Mother Bear, Shekinah—Feminine Wisdom, Sophia, Queen of Heaven, the Source of All Life, The Goddess in all her forms, a Woman in Labor, Compassionate Counselor.

These are only a few descriptions and our definition—the story we tell ourselves about God from our own experiences— informs our ability to fall into God—into the Divine arms— which is to surrender to God's Will for absolute good in our lives. Falling involves surrender and means giving ourselves to God completely.

Christian mystic Julian of Norwich gave herself to God. She lived in England in the 14th century and she asked God directly why he had created the world. The answer came back to her in ecstatic whispers:

> You want to know your Lord's meaning in what I have done? Know it well, love was His meaning. Who reveals it to you? Love. What did he reveal to you? Love. Why does he reveal it to you? For love.

For Julian, God was something to eat, drink, breathe, and see everywhere, as though she were an infatuated lover. Yet since the Divine was her lover, she was elevated to cosmic heights, where the whole universe was, she said, "a little thing, the size of a hazelnut, lying in the palm of my hand."[1]

Panentheism means that we are in God and God is in us like the wave is in the ocean and the ocean is in the wave. God can be seen everywhere, and most of all, God is love. Meister Eckhart, the great German mystic, addressed the idea of the mysterious God in hiding who is love. He said:

> God is like a person who clears his throat while hiding and so gives himself away. God lies in wait for us with nothing so much as love. Now love is like a fishhook. A fisher cannot catch a fish unless the fish first picks up the hook. If the fish swallows the hook, no matter how it may squirm and turn the fisher is certain of the fish. Love is the same way. Whoever is captured by love takes up this hook in such a fashion that foot and hand,

mouth and eyes, heart and all that is in that person must always belong to God. Therefore, look only for this fishhook, and you will be happily caught. The more you are caught, the more you will be liberated.[2]

When we search for this fishhook, the love of God, where do we find it? It is everywhere present—in every person, every situation, and every moment.

"Excuse me," said a little ocean fish to another fish. "you are older than I, so can you tell me where to find this thing they call the ocean?"

"The ocean," said the older fish, "is the thing you are in now."

"Oh this? But this is water. What I'm seeking is the ocean," said the disappointed fish as he swam away to search elsewhere.[3]

When we can put God first in our lives by "Practicing the Presence of God," and seeing the good, the blessing, in everything, then we take hold of that fishhook called love, surrendering, falling into the Divine Presence. In surrender we stop trying to control everything and say, "Thy will be done"—then all things become possible with God.

Sometimes in surrender we are shattered. The nature of falling means that often we get hurt. It is not that God was absent, but was more like a parent helping us learn to walk. If our parents tried to catch us every time we were attempting to walk as babies, we would never have succeeded. And that first step is necessary, and then the leap, falling into God. Surrendering our whole selves is being caught by the fish-hook of love.

> To love God with one's whole heart means to say a whole-hearted yes to life and all that life brings with it. To accept, without reservations, all that God has ordained for one's life. To have the attitude that Jesus had when he said, "Not my will, but yours be done." To love God with one's whole heart is to make one's own the words: For all that has been, thanks. To all that shall be, yes.[4]

Let us fall into God—fall into the net, the arms, the wings, the comforting presence of the Divine by surrendering to love. Then we will discover that God was never hiding, but was there all the time, simply waiting.

Falling into God

Prayer

In prayer, tell God that you surrender yourself fully and ask for His/Her help in letting go and letting God's Will be done. Affirm: *"Thy Will Be Done."*

Meditation

Sit quietly in silence and relax by inhaling and exhaling peace at least three times. Practice surrendering your fears and worries to God. Imagine a Divine Being listening to your concerns and filling you with greater light each time you express yourself.

Physical Activity

Take a walk and imagine a Divine Being with you. (Buddha, Jesus, Mary, or another that you love). With each step reflect on their comforting presence.

Journaling

Write about your experiences in meditation and walking. Describe your concept of God. Where did it come from? How has it evolved from your early teachings?

Stage Two
ENGAGEMENT
—From Uncertainty to Intention—

Experience

Intense love for God

Commitment to conscious transformation

Enhancement of power through ecstasy and vision

Challenge

Cultivation of humility

Danger

Inflation of the ego

Process

The burning away of the ego through overcoming
the temptation of worldly power

Dark night of the soul

Practice

Continued prayer, meditation, study

Remaining self-aware, humble, and awestruck by
God, while unimpressed by any phenomenal
experiences

"The stage of engagement is always characterized by a......series of visions, ecstasies, and illuminations that tremendously expand the seeker's knowledge of his or her own identity and tremendously enhance his or her powers."

Harvey explains that we must remember the source of these powers and continue to cultivate our humility. We are invited to want and seek the Divine above and beyond anything. And we may experience temptations in order to know this. The choice to abuse our personal power is ever-present in the process. But as we remain humble and prayerful, the "divine 'I' can be born in all its splendor." ...What is slowly born from the ashes of all the seeker's previous "selves" is the phoenix of divine identity.

Andrew Harvey, *The Direct Path*, 53-57

Chapter 5

ENGAGEMENT

*I*n 1973, after finally graduating from college with a degree in Education, I took a second trip to Mexico, backpacking from Tijuana through Central America. In Panama, while I was waiting to catch a ship for either Peru or Africa, I was called back to Salt Lake City because my mother was once again in the hospital. It was incredibly disappointing to let go of such an exotic adventure in favor of my role as caregiver. Yet on the plane home I felt inexplicably joyful. This only became clear when shortly after my return I was introduced to the man who would become my first husband. It was intense and passionate and from the beginning we experienced a powerful sense of destiny. He was, however, the herald that comes just before the "Call."

One night he took me to a place called the Paracelsus Research Society to introduce me to his teacher, a world-renowned alchemist. This man was known by the name Frater Albertus, and I was so impacted by the meeting that afterward I locked myself in the bathroom and cried for twenty minutes. My body was racked with deep sobs and I could not tell if it was from joy or sorrow. I would not fully understand the reason I was crying for another seven years when I would finally leave him.

I studied the Western Mystery Tradition in his private school within five miles of my childhood home in Salt Lake City. I had never seen it before though I had driven by it often through the years. Only those involved in his "work" knew of it, and there were many who came from throughout the world to attend the courses taught by Frater Albertus. I met everyone who walked through the doors, including Israel Regardie, the author of many esoteric books and secretary of Aleister Crowley, of the Golden Dawn. My husband Rick and I took courses together and I eventually administrated the organization and taught the Astrology section of the three-fold curriculum: Alchemy, Astrology, and Kabbalah. This seemed an honor since I was the first person ever asked to instruct alongside this amazing teacher.

Alchemy, Astrology, and Kabbalah are considered to be part of the Hermetic teachings. The Egyptian god Thoth, called Hermes by the Greeks, was given credit for "The Hermetic Corpus," a collection of works from ancient Egypt that included these three subjects as well as others.

Alchemy is a path of initiation said to be the "Science of Evolution," since it is the study of transmutation, the fundamental changing of one thing into something else. Inner or Mental Alchemy is the process of awakening that takes place in the individual, as the human soul transforms from its lead-like state of ignorance into the gold of enlightenment. Laboratory Alchemy provides the corresponding outer evidence of the inner experience, proving the link between matter and consciousness.

In the beginning stages of Alchemy, the aspirant learns that the symbols of salt, sulphur, and mercury correspond with body, soul, and spirit. A process of separation, purification, and cohobation (unification) occurs within and without, and as the prospective alchemist purifies the various parts of an herb or a metal in the laboratory, so too does one experience the spiritual "refiner's fire."

Though many have scoffed at Alchemy, associating it with turning lead into gold, there is symbolic and physical basis for the idea. The "Philosopher's Stone" is the great prize of the Alchemist, that mysterious achievement in the laboratory, which is known to preserve life, and transmute all other substances. However, it can be obtained only as a result of the fully awakened Self.

Carl Jung, the Swiss Psychiatrist, called this awakening "individuation." He recognized that alchemical work parallels the individuation process. Jung was attracted to Alchemy and its symbols through a series of dreams and their archetypal images. He spent years investigating the subject and claimed that it was the missing key to the complete understanding of his work. Though Jung was not a Laboratory Alchemist, his interpretations of the key stages and symbols, helped to form the basis for Depth Psychology and earned new respect for Alchemy.

To make progress in Alchemy, one must also learn Astrology and Kabbalah.

Astrology is the study that explores the action of celestial bodies upon all of creation. It is the parent of Astronomy and includes both science and art. The science involves the casting of an accurate horoscope (hour view) from an astronomically calculated table of planetary positions, called an ephemeris. The horoscope or chart is determined from the time and place of birth and reveals the promise inherent in the individual. It reflects both possibilities and pitfalls, though free will always prevails.

The art of Astrology includes an interpretation based on both the technical skill of the Astrologer as well as an intuitive ability to synthesize an entire "gestalt" of the person in question. As in Alchemy and the other hermetic teachings, symbols are the important language that tends to invoke deeper mystical awareness.

The symbols in Astrology illustrate the inner meanings of the planets and the twelve signs, which comprise the Zodiac, a 360 degree circle in space, through which the sun and twelve constellations travel from our perspective on earth.

The planets depict the various energies working in our lives, and the signs show where and how those energies manifest, both within and without.

Since symbols are the language of myth, one can say that Astrology is a living mythology that: 1) gives us insight into the depths of our own psyche; 2) provides us with a map to navigate the world; 3) helps us to understand one another, and 4) creates a cosmology for understanding our place in the universe.

Kabbalah develops the idea of cosmology a step further in providing a map called the Tree of Life that has a place for everything in creation. Kabbalah is the well-hidden Jewish mystical tradition. It is one of the great mystery teachings for its multiple layers of symbolic meaning have confounded scholars and readers for centuries. At first, the secret teachings were conveyed orally from master to disciple, with an assumption that the enlightened one would understand. In the twelfth and thirteenth centuries, the Kabbalah was spread by renowned rabbis.

The most important text revealing the secrets, was *The Sefer Yetsirah, The Book of Creation*, written in Palestine somewhere between the third and sixth centuries. We are told how God created the world by means of the twenty-two letters of the Hebrew alphabet and the ten sefirot, living beings embodying the numbers one through ten, through which creation unfolds. The sefirot are also thought of as lights, powers, or archetypes, and represent stages of God's inner life and the divine personality.

The Zohar, The Book of Radiance, by Spanish Jewish mystic Moses de Leon, deepened and promoted the Kabbalistic movement. The opening chapter of Genesis appears to describe the creation of the world, but it alludes to a more primal beginning—the emanation of the sefirot, and their emergence from the Infinite, or Ein Sof, the transcendent God.[1]

Daniel Matt said,

> In a sense Kabbalah represents "the revenge of myth," its resurgence after being attacked for centuries, after being pronounced dead by rationalist philosophers. The kabbalists appreciate the profundity of myth and its tenacious appeal.
>
> From above to below, the sefirot depict the drama of emanation, the transition from Ein Sof to creation. In the words of Azriel of Gerona, "They constitute the process by which all things come into being and pass away." From below to above, the sefirot constitute a ladder of ascent back to the One. The union of (the masculine and feminine forms of God) gives birth to the human soul, and the mystical journey begins with the awareness of this spiritual fact of life. Shekhinah (Divine Feminine) is the opening to the divine: "One who enters must enter through this gate." Once inside, the sefirot are no longer an abstract theological system; they become a map of consciousness.[2]

During this time that I was immersed in these subjects and was helping to assist my teacher, I had one of the most profound mystical visions of my life. One night I had been meditating upon the fool card in the Tarot deck. It is associated with the number zero and represents the letter Aleph in the Hebrew alphabet, which refers to limitless light. As I was drifting off to sleep I had a vision that was unlike an ordinary dream. I was in a great circle of silence with Jesus. Around this circle I could see people pressed against an invisible barrier, their faces contorted with screaming and crying. I realized that it was suffering humanity, but I was enclosed in a protective circle of utter silence. I was following behind Jesus, whose hair was a deep chestnut color, and whose robe was made of pure light. It was otherworldly—a light that I have not seen in this realm. The circle then turned on its side and became like a giant roulette wheel. I realized that all of the prophets of the ages were on this wheel and whichever one remained after the spin of the wheel was the prophet of this age—my personal prophet, as well. Then the wheel settled back on its side, and the vision ended as it began, where I was back in the circle with Jesus, and I knew he was the chosen one. To this day I can go to that place when I need utter silence and stillness, and I can remember that deep peace and sense of protection.

Frater Albertus was an outer expression of that comforting presence. He was a beloved teacher and healer who took my husband, Rick, and me under his wing. We felt blessed for the amazing teachings and the opportunity to study so closely with him when so many had to travel around the globe for just a short visit with him. He was a master of the deepest esoteric tradition and was held in high regard by those who investigated such mysteries. Sometimes when I listened to his meditations or watched him heal someone I felt such gratitude for his conscious awareness and presence in my life.

Who can say where the unraveling began? Was it when he promised my husband a job at his laboratories so that I could attend graduate school? In my first week of classes Rick was also expecting his first paycheck and was told after the fact that there would be no salary but that it was to his spiritual advantage to volunteer for awhile. Or was it when I went to the grocery store with my teacher several times and noticed him slip an apple in his pocket without paying for it? Or was it after my husband had moved away when he caught me by surprise in a back office and placed my hand on his penis whispering that he had been waiting for me for lifetimes? It was all of that and much more that cannot even be named. There were friendships lost, spiritual soul sisters who became jealous, for each one was hearing the same whispers in secret meetings. It was a long, slow unraveling that intensified and gathered speed toward the end. The shattering of my illusions did not happen overnight. It took years for me to accept the reality that he was in fact the wolf in sheep's clothing and was ultimately involved in the destruction of my marriage through subtle and devious undermining.

After the heartbreak of a marital separation, I discovered I was pregnant, and then my teacher made his move. Vulnerable and wounded, I was a perfect candidate for mental programming and possession. Frater Albertus began trying to convince me that I was his "twin soul." This concept that there is one perfect other half for each one of us had long appealed to my romantic nature, and became a dangerous hook for manipulating me during a time of great loss. I would often awaken in the mornings knowing that he had been speaking to me from a distance while I slept. Later he would corroborate this by actually repeating something from the night. When I asked what he was doing, he responded that he was "clearing the channels for my higher connection."

Before my son's birth and the ensuing psycho-spiritual ordeal, I experienced another powerful vision. When I was six months pregnant I developed appendicitis and struggled to treat it with natural methods. I tried diet and acupuncture and partial chiropractic treatments, all to no avail. Wracked with pain during sleepless nights, I knew that I would have to resort to surgery, which terrified me. One night I read the words of Jesus in the New Testament and then went through Edgar Cayce's book about Jesus. When I climbed into bed I was filled with His Presence, and I had a vision. I was standing in a great hall waiting for Jesus, along with a crowd of people. I heard a voice say, "Do not be deceived—you will know him by his eyes." Then a man came out through a doorway and the people went off with him, and I knew it was not Jesus. And I waited alone, and then He came. I knew him by his eyes and he embraced me like a lover. I was enfolded in love and bliss and passion. I awoke the next morning fully healed! The pain has never returned, and I gave birth to my beautiful nine-pound son Christopher Michael three months later in a relatively easy home delivery that took only four and a half hours.

A week after my son's birth Frater Albertus began coming into my dreams, intensifying his seduction. These dreams where he communicated with me went on for many months, and when my son was one year old I returned to work to administrate my teacher's organization. Then his sexual seduction began, for by now he had made himself quite indispensable to me. He had been my support through a time of loss, my spiritual teacher with access to the mysteries, a father figure offering comfort and authority, and now he wanted to be my lover. He was not a handsome man, actually quite the contrary, and he was nearly forty years my senior. That all paled in the presence of his power. I did not resist for I believed him to know more about spiritual matters than I did. I was afraid of being cut off and my hunger was emotional.

During the last few years of my time with Frater Albertus, I ended the sexual involvement and still continued to work for him. I suspected he was with another woman and so I began to expand my vision and I fell in love with a man who was also involved in the school of alchemy. When Albert learned of it he manipulated me to end my new relationship. This lasted for several months, but I finally defied him and continued to see my lover for another year amidst great inner turmoil about my teacher.

I broke free from Frater Albertus when I finally woke up. It came gradually as numerous incongruities surfaced through the years and my despair became unbearable. I had many vampire dreams at the time and it felt like my life force was being drained out of me by one who fed off the energy of those around him, especially the women. Several "sensitive" people had called to tell me that I was being psychically attacked. My physical strength was nearly gone; my blood pressure had dropped to 80 over 60 and I was barely able to take care of my son, who was now four years old.

One night I dreamed that I was in an assembly hall with the dark lord. Many of us present wore white robes, but I was watching some converted to black robes before my eyes, and realized that I was in tremendous danger. The dark lord called me forward and told me that he was going to lead me in a dance to the death. I first thought that I had to outsmart him by dancing well. And then a crystal clear thought came within my confused mind, and said, "I don't even have to do this dance. I need to get back to my son." At that instant I felt the rush of a great wind and found myself back in my body aware of my son's voice calling from across the room where he slept. After attending to him I climbed back into bed. For awhile I kept trying to get back to finish the dance, until I realized that I had been rescued somehow. From that moment, my physical strength began to return.

Through the guidance of a psychic friend, two other women and I confronted Frater Albertus together. I was terrified since he was unpredictable. But he played the innocent who was being victimized by others. He begged us for help. Then for the next few days when I was alone with him he tried every tactic imaginable to continue his mental imprisonment. I was actually staying around in an effort to put the office in order for the next employee! In retrospect I cannot understand why it took me so long to actually leave, but I was paralyzed with fear and believed my life to be at risk. Finally on the third day, I fled in terror and despair while he was away from the office.

Utterly devastated, I could barely move for days. Just prior to leaving my teacher, I had also ended my relationship with my lover. It was somewhat irrational due to my confusion and the arrival of another man on the scene who was sent, I believe, for a very brief time to help me wake up. I was in deep grief about all of the loss, but it seemed that I had to release everything in order to free myself.

During this time of hibernation my older sister Cheryl arrived in town from California with her children and a close adult friend named Clark, who was later to become my second husband. We all attended a basketball game at the University of Utah Special Events Center. While sitting there feeling cast back out into the mainstream, devoid of a spiritual home, and quite lost, I became aware of the pain around me within the stadium. The place was crowded with people, and suddenly I was one with their universal suffering. They were all cheering for the game and there I sat, plugged into the great cosmic wound of humankind. I was overwhelmed with compassion for all living beings everywhere, and it was a great effort to keep from weeping. Suddenly everything shifted and I was overcome with joy. Now I was one with the joy and bliss and love of the universe. It was in this moment that I felt my call though I did not know what it was at the time. I had known for seven years that I was actively involved in the "Great Work" of evolution. Now all of that seemed to be gone, but instead, the pain and the bliss of the world were shown to me, and my heart was broken open with a profound compassion. What was I supposed to do? I felt this was happening for a reason, though I would not know for yet another seven years that it would become a call to ministry.

In the meantime nine of us from the former Paracelsus Research Society compiled letters in which we stated our truth, and mailed the packets to Frater Albertus's alchemical organizations in Germany and Australia, as well as to all of his key people. We chose not to leave in silence but to reveal the truth. I received phone calls from people all over the world wanting to confirm the story or to denounce me for my "lies and cruelty."

One day after one of these calls, I was overcome with exhaustion and tried to sleep. Suddenly there was a great pressure on my chest and I felt the presence of Frater Albertus there pinning me down. I broke free and rushed across the room to call for help only to discover that I could not pick up the phone because I was not in my body. I glanced at the clock and paced the room wildly, unable to return. After twenty minutes I found myself back in my body with complete laryngitis and an ear infection.

The terror of knowing that such a thing could happen and that I was still not safe caused me to perform numerous rituals of release and purification and ultimately to move with my son to the Midwest in order to escape everyone associated with the organization.

While in Austin, Texas I finally felt the full power of my wounding. Not only did I grieve the loss of a spiritual teacher and a specific path I thought I was traveling, but the death of my father four years before. He died when I was 29 while I was in the midst of my ordeal, and unwilling to feel the pain of his death, I projected the father figure onto my teacher with his encouragement. Now they were both gone and I cried for the illusion, but even more, for the loss of my flesh and blood father in this lifetime. I was alone in a new state with a young son and I was grieving my father's death and a spiritual rape.

It was then that I called a Unity Minister for help. I had heard of Unity, with my metaphysical interests, but had never attended a Unity Church. The minister cancelled all of his appointments when he heard me sobbing on the phone, and spent the day helping me grieve. He planted seeds that began to dissolve my fear. Once I stopped feeling afraid of my former teacher and giving power to him, my life took a different turn. Though I only attended the Unity Church for several months before I moved away, the compassionate minister had kindled a flame that would continue to grow.

Chapter 6

ENGAGING POWER

One ring to rule them all

One ring to find them

One ring to rule them all

And in the darkness bind them

*T*hese words from *Lord of the Rings* by J.R.R. Tolkien, speak to the ring of power. The dark lord Sauron searches for this ring in order to wield it so that evil may again rule the land. Frodo Baggins, hero and ring bearer, along with his friends—his fellowship—all seek to destroy the ring so that evil will be conquered and light and goodness will prevail.[1]

There is only one problem—in order to destroy the ring Frodo must carry it into the heart of Mordor, the land of the dark lord, and cast it into the fires of Mount Doom. And there is the ever-present danger of the ring that corrupts its bearer over time.

This story is our story—one whose time has come. For the sacred quest is ours. It is our quest for Divine love and authentic power. Like Frodo, the hero, we hold the ring of power, the potential to wield our great creative powers for good or ill.

We must journey into the land of our own ego to cast the ring into the refiner's fire—to release the last vestige of our fears, our greed, our negative issues, our prejudice, and most especially our need for control. We uncover, acknowledge and change the unhealthy parts of our self.

And just like the story, temptations occur right up to the end until we are finally able to make the shift and be transformed.

Along the way we discover friendships, allies to help us on our journey. We realize inner resources we did not know were there. And most of all, we discover love. It is the ring of love that we truly seek—the Holy Grail—the great prize of our true selves. It is the ring for our sacred marriage with the Divine, the union of our personality and our soul and of our male and female sides, into one being of light. In order for a marriage to take place there must first be an engagement—a commitment to the vision, the task, the union.

This is the place in our journey where we move from uncertainty to intention.

Frodo says, "I will take the ring to Mordor though I do not know the way." And his friends, the fellowship say, "We will pledge our lives to protect you."[2]

This is the place where lovers pledge, agreeing to take the next step, to become engaged with intent to marry after a period of trial. In our lives this is where we make a greater commitment to our own spiritual path. We set an intention to go deeper. We long for and seek the Divine above and beyond anything.

I spoke about this subject in my church, and on that particular Sunday, I was scheduled to teach a membership class. I love how synchronicity works since some of the people were making a commitment to their spiritual community, setting an intention for greater involvement. The wonderful result is deeper spiritual growth from the power of becoming engaged.

When a couple becomes engaged it is often announced to the public. Engagement invites community support. Just as Frodo's intention caused the fellowship to join with him, so too does our engagement enlist greater connections with one another. The engagement also invites a deeper realization of the Divine and as a result a greater resistance of the ego. This starts a period of trial where we are tempted to take off the ring of love and put on the ring of power.

Engagement is the phase of the journey where we must go through a dark night in which we are tempted to succumb to the unhealthy parts of ourselves. Before it is won, however, there is temptation and power struggle.

Power struggles are the most prominent characteristic of the human experience. Human history is the chronicle of power struggles between individuals, tribes, races, religions, the sexes, and nations. Every country and culture has its stories of struggles with other countries and cultures. ....Striving to manipulate and control what appears to be outside of us, including other people, is the pursuit of external power.[3]

This pursuit of external power is both our collective and individual temptation. Jesus went through it in his forty days in the wilderness. The devil came and told him to command the stones to become loaves of bread. Jesus told him, "Man shall not live by bread alone, but by every word that proceeds from the mouth of God."

Satan took him to the pinnacle of the temple and said to him, "If you are the son of God, throw yourself down; for it is written, 'He will give his angels charge of you,' and on their hands they will bear you up, lest you strike your foot against a stone.'"

Jesus told him, "Again it is written, 'You shall not tempt the Lord your God."

Satan took him to a very high mountain, and showed him all the kingdoms of the world and the glory of them; and he said to him, "All these I will give you, if you will fall down and worship me."

Then Jesus said to him, "Begone, Satan! For it is written,

'You shall worship the Lord your God and Him only shall you serve.'"

Then the devil left him, and behold, angels came and ministered to him.[4]

To overcome our temptations we can do what Jesus did: 1) He put God first; 2) He spoke truth from his own inner authority using statements of release and affirmation; 3) He acted in accord with his spoken words; 4) Then angels came and ministered to him.

That was certainly my experience when I broke free of my teacher. I told him that God was my source of truth, that I was a servant of the light and that I no longer found light in this place where he was. I told him that I released him and all that in myself was power hungry or greedy or evil. I said that I wished only the highest good for his soul and also for my own. And then I ultimately left. And truly angels did come and minister to me when I was in the depths of despair and sadness. They lifted me out of that place in my psyche and in my life. Now at times I can laugh about it.

I love Mark Twain's experience of temptation when he moved to Carson City, Nevada. He wrote a letter home saying, "This place is a den of iniquity filled with wine, women and song—certainly not a place for a good Presbyterian. Therefore I no longer am one!"[5]

Power struggles occur for our purification because in many ways we feel powerless, and then we try to control, which increases the problem. One way that we give our power away is in our search for a savior. The savior we seek may be in the form of a guru, a teacher, a perfect mate, a home, job, car, money, education, or a muscular body. When we seek a savior, this search takes our attention away from what we really feel and places it on external circumstances. It is important that we call forth our power of discernment and ask, "Is this person, situation, or object the answer to my joy and well being?" It is truly the Christ within that we seek, the ring of love, the prize of the true self.

One of the tragedies of our culture is that we give our power away daily. When we do that we fail to engage true spiritual power. We may choose other people as objects of love and credit them with making us happy. And when they leave us we blame them. A certain amount of money in the bank one day can cause us to feel abundant and prosperous. And the next day we receive an unexpected bill. And what happens then? We have all done it—we get upset and feel less than prosperous.

Many of us have felt disillusioned by giving power to authority figures. It is amazing how we can place people on pedestals. Granted, it is important to have heroes and role models whom we can pattern after, but only for the sake of enhancing our own authentic power. If we project our own power onto another we weaken ourselves. An example of this often typical in our culture is worshipping entertainment figures.

I had a stepdaughter named Shalane from my second marriage. She was a television star on the show *Dallas*, where she played the role of Priscilla Presley's daughter for four or five years, after having acted in previous television shows and winning close to 100 trophies in childhood beauty contests. She had become quite well known among teenage crowds. Shalane lived with her mother but came to visit us in the Northwest one particular Thanksgiving weekend when she was fifteen. She came a day early and was able to visit my son Chris's fifth grade class. He had been telling the other children in the class that his sister was on *Dallas* to no avail. Nobody believed him until the day she walked in and there was stunned silence. Suddenly Chris was vindicated. It was great fun, and she spoke with the class and answered their questions. The best one by far asked in complete sincerity was, "Does Elvis ever visit the set?"

That day new friends carried Chris's saxophone home from school and he was not only believed, but was a new hero for a time. This was actually heartwarming to watch, and I also noticed how young this all begins. We give our power away to those who are more famous, more beautiful, more conscious, or whatever we determine is better than we are.

There have been many times in my life when I have given power to a teacher, a psychic, a minister, a metaphysician, or some other authority whom I believed had more knowledge or conscious awareness than I did. There is a distinct difference between seeking help and guidance and giving away power. The latter means that we attribute authority to another and no longer listen to ourselves, but give credence only to the other person. For example, if you were to take my advice because I am a minister and ignore your own guidance, saying "She must be right because she has the answers," that is giving your power away. It is making yourself powerless.

On the other hand you may read a truth I teach and feel it resonate within your own being as true for you also. And if you feel that inner resonance and you are listening to your own guidance then you are very much aligned with your own power.

You may also hear a truth teaching and perceive it intellectually and not feel it in your heart yet. You will still need to put it to the test and once you have and it is your experience then you become your own authority on it.

It is important that we refrain from giving away power to religious organizations. We must refuse the emotional contagion of the masses and listen to our inner guidance. I believe that churches and organizations should empower people, not rob them of their own worth.

When Jesus was taken before Pontius Pilate after being accused of crimes he did not commit, and Pilate threatened him saying, "Don't you know I have the power to release you or to crucify you?" Jesus responded, "You have no power but that given you by the Father."[6]

No person has power over us unless we give it to them. The only real power is the power of God. We do experience people who are in positional power. There is in our world personal power and positional power. Positional power is the power we are given in society or in a corporate hierarchical structure. And this kind of power may be achieved by means of our skills and talents, by the money we have to buy our position, or by the contacts we have, the people we know.

The other power is personal power and this comes from accessing the "Christ"—the Divine Presence within. The problem arises when people achieve positional power before they are ready for it. If this takes place before they are expressing that Divine Presence in the form of personal power, they can be overwhelmed with their position. One expression of this is that the ego may crave the position at the expense of one's ethical values or spiritual development, and the person thereby becomes corrupt. So it is very important that we engage our personal power, accessing the Divinity within.

Even with all of our best efforts, the various temptations and power struggles we experience plunge us into the "Dark Night of the Soul" because the ego and all of its falsehoods must be overcome. The phrase "Dark Night of the Soul" came to us from the writings of St. John of the Cross, a sixteenth century Roman Catholic mystic and co-founder of the Carmelite Order. His description of this stage of the mystical path elucidates what prophets, mystics, and enlightened ones have taught for centuries. The "Dark Night of the Soul" is the painful and often long ordeal that the aspirant must endure and overcome. It is a terrible time, a devastating period in which

God and meaning are absent. It comes after a first dark night that purifies the senses so they can become the vehicle of the inner Divine Self. Then one is ready for the experience of illumination where the entire creation is seen as a manifestation of light. This is not enlightenment, however, and there must be a second death, the Dark Night of the Soul, which is the death of ego or personal identity.

The despair of this stage can be triggered by life events: a betrayal, the death of a loved one, loss of a job, ending of a relationship, diagnosis of an illness, or simply a deep loss of meaning and absence of joy. The experience of the Dark Night is different than a typical ordeal. One feels abandoned by God, utterly bereft of help or consolation. This "underworld" experience may continue for many months or even years until finally there is a complete annihilation and crucifixion of the false self.

The Biblical story of Job illustrates the way God's grace strips us bare, so that we can die to the old personality. Job laments:

> The life in me trickles away,
>
> Days of grief have gripped me.
>
> At night-time, sickness saps my bones,
>
> I am gnawed by wounds that never sleep.
>
> It has thrown me into the mud
>
> Where I am no better than dust and ashes.
>
> I cry to you, and you give me no answer;
>
> I stand before you, but you take no notice.[7]

Everything is taken from Job until his only choice is complete surrender. Only when he is broken and humbled does God comfort him and restore him to even greater fulfillment and joy. Like Job, we must die to everything false, even our concept of God. We are left in a wilderness between an old way of being and the growth towards a new state of consciousness. It is now that we must lose our life to find it as we give up everything to become a purified vehicle for the expression of God. The intensity of this death requires utter dependence on a God that is beyond all that we have ever imagined.

Evelyn Underhill in her great work, *Mysticism*, elaborates on this stage of the path:

> The great contemplatives, those destined to attain the full stature of the mystic, emerge from this period of destitution, however long and drastic it may be, as from a new purification. It is for them the gateway to a higher state. But persons of a less heroic spirituality, if they enter the Night at all, may succumb to its dangers and pains. This 'great negation' is the sorting-house of the spiritual life. Here we part from the "nature mystics," the mystic poets, and all who shared in and were contented with the illuminated vision of reality. Those who go on are the great and strong spirits, who do not seek to *know*, but are driven to *be*.[8]

The Dark Night of the Soul is the final period of testing, and those who make it through have won a great battle. Each of us has the power to do so and can find courage in the words of Jesus when he told us over and over again, "The Kingdom of heaven is within you. These things and even more you can do—even greater things than I."[9]

Charles Fillmore, co-founder of Unity said, "When one is developing out of mere personal consciousness into spiritual consciousness we begin to train deeper and larger powers. We send our thoughts down into the inner centers of our organism and through our word quicken them to life. Where before our powers have worked in the personal, now they begin to expand and work in the universal."[10]

When we pass through the Dark Night and engage our true spiritual power—Christ Consciousness, we no longer need to give our power away by projecting it onto others. We no longer need to have positions of importance. And ironically, when we have surrendered the need for ego-based power, we then tend to have greater influence. Our humility allows us to become transparent that we may be infused with the power of God.

DIVINE GUIDANCE

At this point in the framework of the path it is important to discuss three essential aspects of divine guidance: discernment, synchronicity, and dream work.

DISCERNMENT

I can stress the importance of achieving greater personal power and following one's guidance, however, discerning the truth is not always an easy task. Discernment is actually a spiritual power that can be developed. Ironically, we often do not attain it until we have lost our innocence in the type of betrayal that occurs on the spiritual path. A child will avoid a hot stove by listening to his or her parent or if not, by painful experience. Because we are in a state of amnesia, or forgetfulness about our Divine nature, we may not initially heed the guidance that is all around us, thus falling prey to the dangers on the path.

Much is said about these dangers in traditional religions but tends to be downplayed in the New Thought movements. The latter often teach that evil is not real. I believe that is true in the ultimate sense—that God is the Only Presence and Power in the Universe, and that there is no opposing equal force for God is beyond opposites. However, in the relative plane of existence, this changing reality that we experience daily, there is without question a collective ego that we can call evil. Even in New Thought it is equated with ego, however, the archetypal aspect of it is ignored.

It is true that evil can be a label for different perspectives. What may seem evil to one person, may in fact be a noble religious act for another. We cannot condemn another person for his or her beliefs, but we can discern the true from the false. We can ask to know God's Will for Absolute Good.

I appreciate Scott Peck's definition of evil, which is "militant unconsciousness." He elaborates:

> There really are people and institutions made up of people, who respond with hatred in the presence of goodness and would destroy the good insofar as it is in their power to do so. They do this not with conscious malice but blindly, lacking awareness of their own evil—indeed, seeking to avoid any such awareness. As has been described of the devil in religious literature, they hate the light and instinctively will do anything to avoid it, including attempting to extinguish it. They will destroy the light in their own children and in all other beings subject to their power.
>
> Evil people hate the light because it reveals themselves to themselves. They hate goodness because it reveals their badness; they hate love because it reveals their laziness. They will destroy the light, the goodness, the love in order to avoid the pain of such self-awareness....[11]

I wrestled with the idea of evil during the time I was leaving my spiritual teacher. I had confronted it for the first time in my life, and I could not believe the insidiousness of the force that I experienced.

Andrew Harvey spoke of the same deep soul searching after his devastating experience with his former guru, Mother Meera. I could identify with his awareness that there had been many warnings and signs, including those from the mystics.

He mentioned in St. John of the Cross' "The Ascent of Mount Carmel," how saints distinguished between holy and evil visions; Ramakrishna's teaching about the temptation of abusing occult powers on the path; and Rumi's belief that many of the masters of his day were "black magicians."[12]

We can become too complacent where evil is concerned, just as we are with injustice, which can certainly be a form of evil. In my wrestling I came to know that in the One Mind each of us has access to both good and evil. We contain both dark and light, and we all have the potential to choose. I kept praying to God for the answer. Was my teacher an evil person? Had he been conscious and intentional in his behavior or was he just an unconscious pawn of the dark side? Was there really a dark side?

My answer came through a book. One day in the midst of my continual prayer for insight, I looked at my bookshelf and a book called *Initiation* by Elisabeth Haich was glowing. The book had been on my shelf for three years and I had not yet read it. I began leafing through the pages and found it to be an autobiography describing a Swiss yoga teacher's spiritual path. I was astounded by her description of a manuscript that she found as an answer to her prayers after a long and lonely path.

> The manuscript told about a secret spiritual order that was as old as the earth itself. Without any external, visible form of "membership," the order was constantly taking in neophytes who came in contact with it without

actually knowing anything about it. This "coming into contact" occurred when a person reached such a state of development that he completely gave up his own person and dedicated his entire life to alleviating the sufferings of others. Whenever a person has reached this decision, a member of the secret order gets in spiritual touch with him, or rather the individual who has decided to give up his person and thus has reached universal love has reached a stage in his development such that he automatically responds to the vibrations flowing among the members of this secret spiritual fraternity. First he hears within himself the voice of the spiritual leader and guide, warning him about the difficulties, dangers and consequences of his decision. If he still sticks to his decision, this "order" which exists to help humanity climb up out of chaos, accepts him as a member.

At first he is on probation without actually knowing it. This probationary period begins immediately and for *seven long years* the neophyte is left completely on his own. During this time he has no contact with the order, no matter how much he may desire and seek it. But the various tests he must pass come one after the other. Seven of them relate to the human virtues: becoming free of (selfish) sensuality, vanity, anger, covetousness, envy, (greed)—then on the other side, the ability to withstand outside influences.

If he passes all of these tests in spite of being entirely on his own, and if he sticks by his decision, he is considered ready to begin his work and is definitely accepted within the order. On the very same day, he learns about his acceptance through an "apparent" coincidence. From then on he receives thorough training and, simultaneously, specific tasks. At first these tasks are easy, and as he performs them satisfactorily, they become progressively more difficult. The tasks are very different. Some neophytes must work in public, others behind the scenes. Some roam the countryside as beggars, others are very rich. In either case they must fulfill their duties. Some work as assistants of famous discoverers, others as writers or lecturers. Some hold positions of great worldly power, while others may hold down jobs as workmen in huge factories. It can even happen that two members of the order *appear* to be working against each other. Such persons are not permitted to reveal in any way at all that they belong together and are in contact with each other. Sometimes they are celebrated and enjoy tremendous popularity; at other times they may live in abject misery and be subjected to privations and degradations. They must fulfill all their tasks in a completely free and impersonal manner, simply as servants within the great plan. And as they perform their tasks, they must bear *full responsibility for their each and every act!* They receive their assignments, but they must figure out themselves how to carry them out in complete awareness of the responsibility they bear for everything they do. The higher they rise, the greater their responsibility.

*Anyone who refuses to bear the responsibility for his acts
and his work, and tries to unload this responsibility on
another member of the order,* anyone who does not recognize his work as his own, personally chosen task but
tries to make it appear that he is acting on the instruc-
tions of the order or as a spiritual tool of a member of
the order—such a person is a traitor and instantly loses
all contact with the order. He does not know, however,
that he has lost contact, and it is possible for him to go
on for years believing himself to be a co-worker within
the order. Such persons are used by the order to test
other people and find out whether they accept and follow false prophets or whether they have progressed far
enough in thinking independently and reaching their
own decisions so that they weigh every word they hear
and only accept it after it has passed examination. Those
who follow false prophets are still blind, allowing themselves to be led by blind, and both fall by the wayside.[13]

This information came to me for a reason at a very painful time of inner soul-searching. I felt that it was an answer
to my prayers. Frater Albertus had been given a special work
and he had lost contact. He abused his powers by violating
many of the basic virtues and he did not take self responsibility but often made reference to a guide who was direct-
ing him from a secret order. He became corrupt and in that
sense was unconscious of his own evil. He had aligned himself with it and had become one with the dark side. I believe
he was a black magician, and he was also used by the light

to test the neophyte to see if he or she would follow the false prophet. When I realized this I felt the Grace of God and gratitude that somehow I was not alone and that I had been guided and protected.

Years later in a conversation with my former husband, Rick, I learned that he had attended an Alchemical Conference in Chicago. He had spoken to the renowned French Alchemist who was the keynote speaker and told him that he had studied with Frater Albertus many years before. The Alchemist responded, "Oh he was cut off—the brotherhood cut him off."

This was a startling and unexpected confirmation for me, and once again reminded me about grace and also the importance of discernment.

SYNCHRONICITY

Many people use synchronicity as their process of discernment. These meaningful coincidences, however, should only be confirmation for what is a deeper alignment with Divine Guidance. A synchronistic event is a coincidence with a subjective meaning for the person involved. The meaning generally invokes strong feelings and often a numinous awareness, as though one were in the presence of the Divine.

One example of this was an experience I had while living in Arizona. One Sunday I gave a lesson in my church about the archetype of the Lover and the many ways we can express our love. I spoke most specifically about loving the animal kingdom. After church I drove home, came out of my garage, and there standing at my front door was a peacock! It is not often that peacocks show up at one's front door, particularly in Arizona. To some this may not have seemed very important. But for me it had personal meaning since I had just spoken about the archetype of the Lover and the importance of loving animals, and I happened to know that the peacock was often associated with Hera, the Greek Goddess of love and marriage. The "coincidence" had subjective meaning and was certainly numinous since I felt like I had been visited by the Divine.

Often people take synchronistic experiences as signs, guidance, or answers to prayer. It is most certainly true that they can be and tend to direct one to new doorways of opportunity or change. However, even then, there will always be an inner voice—a still small voice—that guides us if we listen. It is the voice of discernment and it will confirm or contradict synchronicity.

I had a relationship that appeared at a time when I wanted a change in my work and my life. It seemed perfect, and the events that surrounded our meeting were all synchronistic. Early in the experience, however, my inner voice said, "It's too soon." I knew this referred to the fact that he was only recently divorced. But because of all the signs I plunged in anyway, changed my work, my residence, and committed myself to this person. It ended up becoming one of the most difficult relationships of my life. A year and a half later, I returned alone to the town and job I had left. It was a long circuitous journey in which I gained new self awareness along with a deep wound.

Was it a mistake to follow the synchronistic signs? When we are on the verge of a new journey that involves choice, the inner voice of discernment is always present guiding us. If we listen we may experience the next phase with less suffering and trouble. When we do not listen, the journey may be more painful but filled with great lessons.

Did I make a mistake following a false spiritual teacher? I had the same guidance early on in that relationship as well. A voice said to me, "I represent the authorities and this is not the time and place for this relationship." But I ignored it and proceeded since I did not yet understand or trust my own discernment. If I had listened perhaps I would have been ready for more advanced teachings and greater joy. I chose the more difficult path and to this day I believe that Frater Albertus was my greatest teacher though I wish I had never met him. There was great personal cost and I also learned so much that has been invaluable.

DREAM WORK

Another essential form of guidance on the journey is the gift of our dreams. Every single night we dream, though we may not remember. When we cultivate the memory of our dreams and the spiritual practice of dream work we have an invaluable tool of awareness. This practice provides, in fact, the most reliable method of accessing the unconscious and the soul's true intention.

John Sanford, Jungian analyst and Episcopal Priest tells of his four year old daughter's first reported dream. She rushed into the kitchen, her eyes wide with excitement and announced, "Daddy, I had a story last night; it was a bear story—and I was in it too!"[14]

I love that idea of a nighttime story for it is true that dreams are stories. They come from the realm of imagination and they include characters and symbols which convey meaning to us. It is said that we are the creatures who think in stories.

Joseph Campbell, the mythologist, said, "We will come to know that all of life is a story." There is only one Great Story and one Hero or Heroine wearing many masks— many costumes.[15] Even our earth has its own story. I once heard Mathematical Cosmologist Brian Swimme say, "The universe is a story. It is not a static thing—but an unfolding story."

Dreams are stories that heal. They help us see where we are living in outdates stories, and they come to guide us, to wake us up, to heal us, and to transform our lives. They do this for us personally and collectively. There comes a time as we work on our own issues, when we realize that our personal concerns are part of a larger story. We can no longer separate ourselves from the destiny of the planet. This is a time in history when it is essential that we do all we can to awaken personally and collectively for the good of our species and our world. Working with our dreams is a very important spiritual practice for this awakening.

Carl Jung, the Swiss Psychoanalyst, had a dream in 1909. This dream was both personal and collective for it guided him personally, and it had a message that was for everyone. It led him to the concept of the collective unconscious. Jung related this dream:

I was in a house I did not know, which had two stories. It was "my house." I found myself in the upper storey where there was a kind of salon furnished with fine old pieces in rococo style. On the walls hung a number of precious old paintings. I wondered that this should be my house and thought "not bad." But then it occurred to me that I did not know what the lower floor looked like. Descending the stairs I reached the ground floor. There everything was much older, and I realized that this part of the house must date from about the 15th or 16th century. The furnishings were medieval; the floors were red brick. Everywhere it was rather dark. I went from one room to another, thinking "Now I really must explore the whole house." I came upon a heavy door and opened it. Beyond it, I discovered a stone stairway that led down into the cellar. Descending again, I found myself in a beautifully vaulted room which looked exceedingly ancient. Examining the walls, I discovered layers of brick among the ordinary stone blocks and chips of brick in the mortar. As soon as I saw this I knew that the walls dated from Roman times. My interest by now was intense. I looked more closely at the floor. It was a stone slab and in one of these I discovered a ring. When I pulled it the stone slab lifted and again I saw a stairway of narrow stone steps leading down into the depths. These, too, I descended, and entered a low cave cut into the rock. Thick dust lay on the floor, and in the dust were scattered bones and broken pottery, like remains of a primitive culture. I discovered two human skulls obviously very old and half disintegrated. Then I awoke.[16]

From this dream Jung discovered his hypothesis of the collective unconscious; he saw the house in this dream as an image of the psyche with consciousness being represented by the salon on the first floor, the ground floor for the first level of consciousness, and the deeper he went as being more alien, until finally the long uninhabited prehistoric cave, which he saw as signifying past times and past stages of consciousness. Thus the unconscious was seen to have both a personal and impersonal or collective aspect.

Through this collective unconscious each individual is linked with his or her own past and the past of the species. This is the realm of the archetypes. Carl Jung coined the term to mean a universal pattern or image in the collective unconscious. Plato called them the forms. Charles Fillmore, co-founder of Unity called them Divine Ideas in the Mind of God.

Carl Jung wrote extensively about dreams, and there are many other perspectives and ways of interpreting dreams, but Jung's language and concepts are often used by dream workers, so I will discuss it briefly.

Archetypes are like the story characters in our psyche. They symbolize different powers within us, such as faith, strength, wisdom, order, joy, and others. Jung gave them names such as: The wise old man, as a universal symbol of wisdom; the great mother, as a goddess figure of birth and esoteric secrets; the hero/savior, as the Messiah figure. These characters are found throughout the world. They show up with different names in different cultures, but their meaning and purpose is the same, and they have existed through time, thus, they are archetypal.

It is important to be aware of some of these figures as we work with our dreams. Some of the ones that show up frequently include: the Shadow—it will often be a figure of the same sex who is not very nice, or it can appear as a frightening figure that we do not want to face. Often shadow dreams are nightmares that come to ask us to pay attention to the disowned parts of our self—which is what the Shadow is.

For example, there was a man who was very ill, and he kept having nightmares in which he was running from a frightening monster. Nightmares always come to get our attention. When he worked with a dream therapist, it was revealed that he was ignoring a childhood tragedy that needed healing. As he became willing to face his issues through continued dreams and personal work, his illness went away. Finally, he had a dream where he stopped and faced the monster and was willing to die. At that point the monster smiled and walked away. He had faced up to his shadow, the unconscious disowned parts within trying to get his attention. He became willing to die to his old self and so the shadow within probably saved his life.

His dreams led like a thread from the labyrinth of his own thoughts to renewed healthy attitudes, to a free conscience and reconstructed relationships. There was a Divine intelligence within his psyche that was responsible for these meaningful dreams.

Charles Fillmore said, "Instead of treating the visions of the night as idle dreams, we should inquire into them, seeking to know the cause and the meaning of every mental picture. Every dream has origin in thought, and every thought makes a mind picture. The study of dreams and visions is an important one, because it is through these mental pictures that God communicates with us in a certain stage of our unfolding."[17]

Charles Fillmore was living in Kansas City with his wife, Myrtle, and their three children. Because of Myrtle's tuberculosis, they were about to move from Kansas City back to Colorado where the climate was better for her. Then he had an unusual experience which he related:

> I had a strange dream. An unseen voice said, "Follow me." I was led up and down the hilly streets of Kansas City and my attention called to localities I was familiar with. The presence stopped and said: "You will

remember having had a dream some years ago in which you were shown this city and told you had a work to do here. Now you are being reminded of that dream and also informed that the invisible power that has located you will continue to be with you and aid you in the appointed work." When I awoke, I remembered that I had such a dream and had forgotten it.[18]

It proved to be fortunate that they stayed because events unfolded that changed their lives and began the Unity Movement.

Another dream figure that often shows up is the anima, or feminine figure in a man's dream, or the animus or masculine figure in a woman's dream. These dream characters come to tell us about our psyche as well.

When I had the difficult relationship that I spoke of earlier under the heading of Synchronicity, I began having a recurring dream that would not leave me alone for over a year. Recurring dreams, like nightmares, come to get our attention.

In the dream, *I am still trying to move from the Santa Cruz house I had just left in waking reality. I have a day and a half to clean it, pack everything, and move out. I am doing it all alone, and I am concerned that I am not going to complete it in time.* There were many different variations of the dream over the year, but the theme was always the same. Sometimes it would come nightly for weeks. Then it would leave for awhile and return in force. It so haunted me that I sought Jeremy Taylor's help, a dream worker and mentor, whose insights were profound. (See *Chapter 13*)

This dream was symbolic of the current relationship, and some of the details revealed the animus or male within, which the man in my life symbolized. The dreams indicated I had a day and a half to clean the house, and the relationship lasted exactly a year and a half. I was cleaning alone, and my perception was that for many months I was the only one in the relationship engaged in any inner work or spiritual effort.

There was a specific night in waking reality where I surrendered to God and said, "I cannot do this anymore—I do not know what to do—I give it to you. Please help me!" That night I dreamed that the landlord of the house appeared and took the keys back from me. He said, "Don't worry about anything, I will finish the job." That ended my recurring dream.

From that point in waking life, the relationship came completely unraveled and ended in a relatively positive way through a helpful attitude on both sides and a final forgiveness ritual at the end.

Interestingly, I took a trip to Santa Cruz after that, before I moved there a second time, and visited my former landlord in waking life. He had just gotten married, and the tenant in the house where I had lived had just gotten divorced. There was a fascinating intersection of the dream world and waking reality. Like the tenant in the house, my relationship with the man ended, but like the landlord, recently married, I integrated aspects of myself through the experience.

The landlord in the dream world who takes the keys back from me is a symbol of the Self. The Self is the Divine figure, the Christ, the realized being within us, whom we aspire to. I had finally let go of control and surrendered, and my dream reflected it, and then everything unfolded in perfect Divine Order.

To this day I am grateful for that dream that was relentless in its guidance. I have been led by dreams into every church I have served, and dreams continue to inform me that I have a Divine Presence helping me, as we all do.

We are healed and guided by dreams personally and collectively. The Native Americans call the collective dreams "big dreams" because they are for the people, for the greater community.

Black Elk had a big dream when he dreamed of the great hoop and prophesied for his people. Einstein dreamed of the theory of relativity. Elias Howe had a dream in which he saw the answer to his creative dilemma about how to make the sewing machine. His problem was solved, and thus began the industrial revolution.[19]

Theologian Matthew Fox wrote a book based on a dream in which the final refrain said, "Your mother is dying," and he knew it was a "big dream" about the devastation of Mother Earth. His book speaks to that as well as to the possible cure and resurrection. He said,

Humanity has the power and responsibility to increase the glory that is the living presence in the cosmos. And thus we are all called to birth the Cosmic Christ in self and society. We are called to radiate the Divine Presence to with and from one another—to be bearers of the new paradigm, this living cosmology and its new wineskins; we are called to be patterns that connect and mirrors reflecting the image of God.[20]

This is what Carl Jung said about our journey to individuation or wholeness, and what Charles Fillmore taught about becoming Christ Conscious. It is what all mystical traditions emphasize—the awakening of the Self and its greater effect on the collective whole.

In order to wake up and become your own authority I invite you to invoke the power of dreams and to write them in the journal you are keeping as you read this book.

1) When you go to sleep, ask to have a dream and to remember it in the morning.

2) Have paper and pencil ready or a small tape recorder.

3) Do not move when you awaken, but pause and remember and then write or record your dream.

4) List the images and their possible meanings for you personally.

5) If an image does not make sense go into meditation and hold it in your mind. Keep seeing it until different meanings come to you.

6) Attempt to summarize an interpretation and then continue to stay receptive to more layers of meaning.

Every night there is a story or sacred narrative unfolding for our wholeness. It is God's special language, from the realm of imagination, rich and exciting to discover.

Dreams are stories that come to guide us, teach us, heal us, and to transform our lives. Let us embrace their power and as we do, we awaken ourselves for the benefit of all creation.

The three forms of Divine Guidance mentioned: discernment, synchronicity, and dreams, are important ways to access the Will of God and discover our own personal power. With each one it is essential that we turn within and listen to the truth of our being.

Eckhart Tolle tells of a beggar who had been sitting by the side of the road for over 30 years. One day a stranger walked by.

"Spare some change?" mumbled the beggar, mechanically holding out his old baseball cap.

"I have nothing to give you." Said the stranger. Then he asked, "What's that you're sitting on?"

"Nothing," replied the beggar. "Just an old box. I have been sitting on it for as long as I can remember."

"Ever look inside?" asked the stranger.

"No." said the beggar. "What's the point, there's nothing in there."

"Have a look inside," insisted the stranger.

The beggar managed to pry open the lid. With astonishment, disbelief, and elation he saw that the box was filled with gold.[21]

Until we stop looking outside of ourselves for our security and validation and until we stop the ceaseless demands of the ego, we do not recognize the magnificent treasure that is within. It is nothing less than the very Kingdom/Queendom of God to which we are all heirs.

So I invite you to become engaged—set an intention to be an expression of authentic spiritual power in the world. Listen to your Divine Guidance and follow it, and then the ring of love shall be yours.

Engaging Power

Prayer

Pray to God for greater discernment and protection.

Pray daily: *"The light of God surrounds me, the love of God enfolds me, the power of God protects me, the presence of God watches over me. Wherever I am, God is, and all is well."*

Meditation

Sit quietly in silence and relax. Imagine walking into "Mordor," the darkness within, and facing those parts of your ego that fear, condemn, criticize, and control. Ask that they be revealed and that you be healed. Locate and nurture the parts of yourself that are: loving, caring, creative and joyful. Imagine yourself blessed as you are filled with spiritual power.

Physical Activity

List those parts of your ego that you wish to release and then burn the paper. Take a bath or shower, knowing that you are being cleansed, while reflecting on what you love about yourself.

Journaling

Note your experiences from the above exercises and also begin to record your dreams and other forms of guidance.

Chapter 7

ENGAGING FAITH

"Faith is the assurance of things hoped for, the conviction of things not seen."[1]

$\mathcal{E}$ngagement is the place in the journey where we make a commitment and set an intention for something we want to see happen. *We move from uncertainty to intention.* A couple becomes engaged with an intention to marry, or we decide to become more actively engaged in the spiritual search with intention for deeper growth and service.

When we understand spiritual law, we know that by setting such an intention not only do we invoke the temptation to project and abuse power, but we also invite deeper faith. And it is our faith that sustains us through the dark night of the soul.

One of the reasons I came to love Unity was the story and example of faith. Charles and Myrtle Fillmore, co-founders of Unity knew about the power of faith and intention. They wrote a covenant in 1892 that expresses their faith:

> We, Charles Fillmore and Myrtle Fillmore, husband and wife, hereby dedicate ourselves, our time, our money, all we have and all we expect to have, to the spirit of truth, and through it to the Society of Silent Unity. It being understood and agreed, that the said Spirit of Truth shall render unto us an equivalent for this dedication, in peace of mind, health of body, wisdom, understanding, love, life, and an abundant supply of all things necessary to meet every want without our making any of these things the object of our existence. In the presence of the conscious mind of Christ Jesus, this 7th day of December A.D., 1892. Signed Charles and Myrtle Fillmore.[2]

The Fillmores dedicated themselves to God; they made a commitment, set an intention, and activated their faith by expecting results. They very much believed in God and wanted to help others receive God's blessings, and they had the power of a deep understanding faith.

They were committed souls who believed in the evolution and transformation of humankind. Charles Fillmore once described Unity's purpose to be the spiritualizing of humanity. This aspiration lies at the heart of all spiritual traditions, and is a significant mission to align with. An intention for

the spiritual awakening of everyone certainly takes an activation of our faith.

Faith increases as we evolve in a spiral progressing from
hope, to blind faith, to understanding faith. When we practice
developing it through prayer and meditation and also through
small demonstrations, it prepares us to meet the challenge of
various ordeals, including the dark night of the soul.

There is a wonderful story in Greek mythology about
Prometheus, who stole fire from the gods and made them
very angry. So he warned his brother Epimetheus that the
gods might be taking revenge and so not to accept any gifts
from them. But "Zeus had created a wonderful gift for the
purpose of bringing misery to man forever after. It was the
first woman." As we can see, this idea that woman came to
torment man is not only found in the description of Eve in
the Book of Genesis, we find it in other stories and myths as
well, and it is a false myth!

This particular woman was called Pandora, and Epimetheus
fell in love with her at first sight, and so invited her into his
life. But there was a box which he was given, and she was told
not to open this box whatever she did, but her curiosity got
the best of her. One day she opened the lid, and all of the evils
of the world flew out and went all over the globe. But finally,
after everything flew out, there was one little winged creature
remaining in the bottom, and it was hope. Pandora nestled
the creature against her breast, and so in the darkest times, it
is said that there is always hope in the human heart.

Thus, we begin in hope. And if, for some reason, something is going on in your life and you cannot activate your faith, then hope is the point of beginning. It is that belief and trust that somehow, some way, everything is going to improve and will finally be all right again.

We all have healing needs that call upon our hope and faith because we are part of the human experience. In many of the New Thought teachings, including Unity, people pretend that their problems do not exist. "This is not happening. I do not have any needs. I am fine. This is hell but it's not really hot!" This was especially true in earlier Unity thought; however, in contemporary teachings there is more acceptance of the shadow and the importance of integrating the darkness.

Myrtle Fillmore expressed that truth in her healing. She was dying of tuberculosis at the age of forty, and she did not deny that fact. She faced her illness by focusing on her body and loving it, asking it to forgive her for any mistreatment, sending words of strength and truth to her organs and life centers, and she healed herself. She set an intention for healing and she activated her faith.[3]

Each of us has a healing need as we struggle with universal or personal challenges. Perhaps we long for the healing of our finances with greater prosperity, or a resolution of physical, emotional, or mental illness. We may be suffering in our souls from some past life injury, or attempting to solve a problem in our work or relationships. Some of us may feel that we have never found the right partner in life. And all of us have some fears and concerns about the state of the world at this time. Whatever it might be, we have healing needs. And whenever we are in the realm of hope we are also contending with doubt, because we must develop a deeper understanding faith, which is based on spiritual law.

Blind faith is an instinctive trust in a higher power which we do not necessarily understand how to activate. We pray beseechingly, "Dear God, please help me," and we somehow trust there will be an answer even though we may not recognize its appearance.

For example, a man is trapped in a flood in his home. The water rises past the first level so he goes up to the second level. A boat comes up and the man in the boat says, "Hop on I'll save you." And the man replies, "No thanks, God will save me." The water keeps rising, so the man moves to the third level and the boat returns. The driver of the boat says, "Hop on, I'll save you." The man says, "No thanks, God will save me." The water rises some more and he goes to the roof. The boat returns and once again the driver implores the man to get in. "Hop on, I'll save you." The man refuses, "God will save me."

So the man drowns and goes to heaven. He stands before God, and says, "God, I don't understand. I had faith, why didn't you save me?" And God replies, "Why do you think I sent the boat?"[4]

This is the realm of blind faith. We pray beseechingly, "Dear God, please help me." Somehow we have trust, an instinctive faith, but we do not understand how it works, and we may overlook the answer. Even though blind faith can succeed, there is no conscious activation of spiritual law.

Understanding faith, though, is based on immutable principle. It is the knowledge that God is absolute good—that God's will for us is good, that God is not a punishing God, but a God of love, who wants the very best for us. An understanding faith knows that the desires of our heart are God's will for our good, tapping at the door of our consciousness. As we pray for true spiritual desires and affirm them, applying the law by alignment of our thoughts, our words, and our actions, then we absolutely know and trust that God's will is being done. That is understanding faith.

Healing through the power of faith is addressed in many parables of Jesus, such as this story of the man at Bethesda:

> Now there is in Jerusalem by the sheep gate a pool—in Hebrew called Bethesda, which has five porticoes, and in these lay a multitude of invalids—blind, lame and paralyzed. One man was there who had been ill for 38 years. Now when Jesus saw him and knew that he had been lying there a long time he said to him, "Do you want to be healed?" [And that's the important question.] The sick man answered him, "Yes, but sir, I have no man to put me into the pool when the water is troubled, and while I am going another steps down before me." And Jesus said to him, "Rise, take up your pallet and walk." And at once the man was healed and he took up his pallet and he walked.[5]

Faith is our "yes" power. The man said, "Yes," and with his answer, he set an intention for healing. It is especially noteworthy that the man had been in this condition for 38 years. This tells us that if we have been in a situation for a long time or find ourselves repeating a pattern, and we begin to lose hope that this can ever change, healing is still possible. Once we make that connection with the Christ or the Divinity within and activate our faith through our intention to be healed, then healing can occur in seemingly miraculous ways.

The Metaphysical Bible Dictionary defines the five porticoes where all of the sick people are resting, as the five senses.[6] When we are functioning in the realm of the five senses, we may have the appearance of illness, but once we move into the healing pool, that inner place of stillness and healing power, and make that connection with Christ Consciousness, then all illness can disappear and we can be healed in a moment.

That is why stories of faith are important for us. I know they exist in all traditions, and I love the fact that the entire Unity movement was founded on faith through the healings of Myrtle and Charles Fillmore. Their story is a moving one regardless of one's religious or spiritual background. Myrtle was healed of tuberculosis when she had been given six months to live at the age of forty and Charles had a skating accident at age ten, where his hip was dislocated, his leg became withered and shrunken, and the infection impacted the hearing and vision on his right side. He was on crutches for months and then wore a steel extension on his leg for many years.

Yet he too activated his faith, as he began to practice meditation and affirmative prayer. At first it was hope, then a blind faith—actually more in the laws of science than God—and finally a deep understanding faith, as results began to occur and he realized how to be a co-creator in his own healing. And he was healed. His vision and hearing returned on his right side and he was able to discard his steel brace and walk with only a slight limp well into his 90's.[7]

Each of us deepens our faith through many eleventh hour experiences, practical demonstrations of the law, and also by the grace of God. From the time I was first called to the ministry it seemed like all the forces of the universe came to test and deepen my faith. I have had to step off the cliff more times than I have ever desired, but it has shown me that I can fully depend on God.

When I first went to ministerial school, my former husband, Clark, my two sons, and I moved from the state of Washington to Missouri. We went without a job because it was a spiritual calling and we trusted. After an extensive search we found a house that was not going to be available for three weeks, so my family of four had to camp in a park for that period of time because we knew no one. My two sons, ages eleven and four at the time, thought it was a grand adventure. Trust children to know the truth and to have an innate faith!

During this period I lost my purse, which on that particular day, contained not only my wallet, but my husband's.

We had no cash, no credit cards, and we were stranded in a new state without friends. After we finally got the cards reinstated, Clark could not find work and so we depleted our money. It was then I prayed in desperation, "God, help us! I do not understand your will. I am here to become a minister so why is this happening?"

I surrendered and finally learned to trust in God with my whole being because there was no other choice. Four churches ended up tithing to me which helped me to complete school. God revealed herself in so many ways, and my faith was deepened in the process and has continued to be through the years of working in the ministry. I call it the "faith business," because that is exactly what it is. But I am getting ahead of my own personal story.

Mahatma Gandhi once said, "This belief in God has to be based on faith which transcends reason...a living immovable faith is all that is required for reaching the full spiritual height attainable by human beings." And he added, "When you find your faith is failing or your body is failing you, and you are sinking, God proves to you that you must not lose your faith and that God is always at your beck and call, but on God's terms, not on your terms."[8]

We become more proficient with understanding faith as we spiral into deeper trust in God. Each demonstration confirms our faith and causes greater surrender to the Will of God.

The Fillmores were tested in their faith when financing the Unity work was a continual struggle in the early days of the movement. But God could not have chosen people more ideally suited to this than Charles and Myrtle Fillmore, because they believed what they taught and they had a powerful faith.

In the early 1900's Unity had grown to a point that their goal for the Unity Society was to buy property and erect a new building. One penny had been donated to begin a building fund, and by 1905 this had only increased to $601. But they did not give up. The building committee found a lot and eight rooms in a house for sale in downtown Kansas City. But the money was not forthcoming, so they prayed and prayed, and still the money did not come. And then one evening one of the Board members stood up and said that he had decided to mortgage everything he had in order to provide Unity with the funds needed in order to buy the lot. This man was not rich, and he had a wife and four small children to support. His business associates tried to discourage him, but this man did not lose one cent, and in a short time was the owner of a much more successful business than he had owned before.

By 1920, the first 58 acres were purchased, and today it includes 1600 square acres. It was the intention and the faith that brought it about, and we can do the same thing in our lives for whatever we require, according to God's Will.[9]

When we activate our faith, we are activating immutable principle. Emilie Cady said,

> There are some things that God has so indissolubly joined together that it is impossible for even him to put

asunder. They are bound together by fixed immutable laws...The mental and spiritual realms are governed by laws that are just as real and unfailing as the laws of the natural world. And certain conditions of mind are so connected with certain results that the two are absolutely inseparable. God, the one creative cause of all things is Spirit, and is the sum total of all good. And there is no good that you can desire in your life which at its center is not God. Affirm the possession of the good that you desire; have faith in it because you are working with Divine law and cannot fail. Do not be argued off your basic principle by anyone and sooner will the heavens fall than you fail to get that which you desire.[10]

Trust in that immutable principle—beginning with hope—then through prayer ask to know that God can be trusted. Set an intention, and affirm that it is already being done.

When the Fillmores made their covenant with God it was in complete expectation that the covenant would be fulfilled. They intended to do their part and had perfect faith that God would do His/Her part.

They believed that if they maintained a consciousness of God as the source of their supply and their health, that prosperity and health could not fail to be theirs. And if the money did not come in, then it was a question of their consciousness being deepened, and they would re-double their efforts in prayer.

Through prayer, each one of us can engage the faith necessary for the spiritual journey, especially as it becomes more challenging. It is essential to be grounded in a deep faith as we invoke the power of light with greater intensity.

Engaging Faith

Prayer

Invoke the Divine idea of faith and ask God to deepen your faith. Moving your arms in broad strokes, sweep affirmations of faith from the top of your head down through your body. As you are sweeping your hands down say, *I am filled with faith. I have faith in God. I have faith in my Self.* Keep repeating, adding other words as you are moved to.

Meditation

Sit quietly in silence and relax. Go within and meditate on the power of faith. Imagine that just as you step off the edge of a cliff, you are lifted by angel's wings. Let yourself go and trust in the ride. Practice surrendering to Spirit.

Physical Activity

Take a faith walk with another person. Blindfold yourself and completely trust that person to lead you where they will with the provision that they will keep you safe and free from harm.

Journaling

Write about your faith and whether your thoughts, words, and actions have been concurrent with the desires of your heart.

Chapter 8

ENGAGING LIGHT

God said "Let there be light!" and there was light.

God saw how good the light was

And God separated the light from the darkness.[1]

*E*ach of us is traveling on a journey into greater light. The problem with engaging light is that we must have the spiritual strength to withstand it. We can invite a sudden kundalini awakening, for example, with the resulting trauma when one is unprepared. "According to ancient seers, the kundalini energy resembles a snake resting (for most of us) at the base of the spine. When it is roused, it raises its head and climbs upward, activating various energy centers (chakras or wheels) as it goes. The student is cautioned to approach this process wearily, for premature awakening can easily lead to imbalance of the system. ...The kundalini experience is associated with enlightened states of consciousness, as a great halo of light envelops the being."[2]

Light tends to also illuminate the ego, and we become vulnerable for temptation according to its specific demands. (See Chapter 6, *Engaging Power*). Many aspirants therefore spend years in training. From the beginning, mystery schools have existed within ancient temples of all cultures. Priests and priestesses throughout the centuries have been initiated into the deeper mysteries—all designed to aid the aspirant in his or her awakening or spiritual enlightenment.

Levels of mastery are attained according to our worthiness of higher knowledge. The greater the light and energy within us, the more potential to use our creative powers for good or ill. Just as you would not hand an untrained person a surgeon's knife and say, "Go perform surgery," so too would you be certain that an initiate on the spiritual path is ready for the power of light he or she will gain with greater knowledge.

World literature abounds with stories of magicians turning away from the light. The magician Saruman the Wise is an example in *Lord of the Rings*. His student, Gandalf, resisted the temptation to abuse power and submit to the dark side. He did not need the attention that the ego demands but was confident of his own power and was grounded in his relationship with the light.[3]

Like Gandalf, we too must overcome the temptations of the ego such as fear, greed, and all those false beliefs that come from a central idea that we are somehow separate from God. The truth is that we are one with God, one with the Divine light that is present in all of creation. We have the potential to be light bearers as we stand in and for the light of truth.

In this station of Engagement we have visions and ecstasies as we begin to see light shining everywhere. It may seem that everything is on fire. And yet we should not allow ourselves to be led astray by phenomena. In the early stages of the path we may think that we have become enlightened, however this is not the case. The visions and awareness help to prepare us, for they are only a fore-shadow of what is to come.

Light is often symbolic of increased conscious awareness. When we do not understand something, we say that we must "bring it to light." If we are confused, we say that our process "needs more light." When a sudden idea reorders our thoughts, we say that the "light came on," and when a person is fully conscious, we say that he or she is "enlightened."[4]

We are continually encouraged to move into the light from the loving guidance and assistance received at each moment of our journey.

> Nasruddin, the fool of the Sufi tradition, had this kind of prompting. He was on the ground searching franti-cally for his keys. A friend walked up to him and asked, "Mullah, what are you searching for?" And Nasruddin replied, "I've lost my keys." And so the friend began to

scour the area as well, on his hands and knees.

Finally, after they had both spent much time with no results, the friend said, "Mullah, can you remember where you might have dropped your keys?" Nasruddin replied, "Yes, I lost my keys down the street near my house." And the friend asked, "Then Mullah, why in the world are we searching here?" And Nasruddin replied, "There's more light here, of course."[5]

We are guided toward the light and we always have choice, and yet we do not want to become afraid of the dark because darkness is not all evil or ego. It is also feminine, silence, the stillness of meditation, and the depth of Mother Earth.

Theologian Matthew Fox said that we are "questers after light, which has resulted in the light bulb, electricity, neon lights. From that came the radio, then television—a new kind of light machine—that combines eyes and ears. And one result is that we have become afraid of the dark. Afraid of no light—of silence and image-lessness. We become greedy for more images, more light, more profits, more goodies."[6]

Our spirituality needs to contain both light and dark, for there is a dark side of the light and there is a light side of the darkness. A Greek myth illustrates this concept:

A youth named Phaethon journeys to the palace of the sun. It is a dazzling radiant place, which mortals usually cannot enter let alone find. So Phaethon enters the throne room and he can hardly see. And the sun asks him, "What is your purpose here?" And he says, "I have come to find out if you are my father as my mother has told me you are."

Well, the sun God removes his burning mantle so the youth can look at him with more ease. And he says, "Yes I am your father and in order to prove it to you, I will take an oath on the River Styx and give you anything you ask of me."

And so Phaethon says, "My only wish is that for one day I can take your place and drive your chariot across the sky."

And in that moment the sun God realizes his terrible folly, but he has taken an oath on the River Styx and cannot break it.

So he says to his son, "I have to keep my promise to you but I must urge you to change your mind. No mortal can drive this chariot of the sun, and no God other than myself can drive this chariot—not even the king of the gods himself.

But the youth is so caught up in the idea of the power and the glory that will be his in this moment, this day, that he refuses to listen. So the Sun God tells him that the ascent with the horses when he reaches the mid-heaven is so high the Sun God does not even like to look down. And the descent is so unbelievable that the Sea Gods are amazed that the sun does not plunge into the sea and disappear forever.

So when Phaethon begins the ascent it is such an incredible exhilaration, but it lasts only for moments because
he loses control of the steeds and when he reaches the
midheaven and begins the descent there is nothing but
terror. The plunge is so great and the horses go completely wild and begin to set fire to the earth. And finally
Mother Earth cries out, and Zeus, the king of the gods
responds by sending his thunder bolt to put the youth
out of his misery and save the earth. [7]

This story urges us to heed the Divine Presence within,
rather than the voice of ego. The images of the sun, of light,
of fire, have long been symbols of Spirit, or God in world
mythology and scripture. In the Greek myth of Phaethon,
the chariot of the sun represents a means by which we enter
into the presence and power of God, and become the Christ.
The most powerful vehicle that we have in our lives to enter
into that light, that presence and power, is prayer and heart-
based intention.

This story of Phaethon tells of a wild ride where the driver
of this chariot loses total control. One must be ready for the
full power of Spirit; this is why the spiritual journey is a step-
by-step process. There are countless stories of individuals who
have unleashed the kundalini power and have burned themselves up. There are many who have tried to have awakening
through drugs and have literally incinerated their circuits.

With prayer we take a practice ride in a chariot. We learn
how to keep control of the reins, how to create heart-based

intentions, how to focus on the light and know our destination, and how to fly to the most ecstatic heights imaginable. We learn how to traverse the waters of engagement before we actually take our sacred marriage vows.

I had a profound experience of prayer when I was in ministerial school. I had moved to the Kansas City area where Unity Village is located and had only been there a week when I received a call that my mother was in the hospital once again. She had been without a manic high requiring hospitalization for at least five years, so I was distraught that it had to happen now. I was in no position to leave and knowing her pattern of recovery very well, felt that it was unnecessary at the present time. Instead, I called her often and stayed in contact with her brother Max who was visiting her regularly. Even though she was not rational, it was a comfort to attempt conversation. After several days, though, my uncle called me in great alarm. He said that mom was very ill and could not leave her bed. She was completely despondent, almost like a "zombie." This had never happened since her illness was mental not physical. When I called the hospital they said that she was very ill and they were trying to determine the problem.

It was then I went into the heart of the Unity Prayer Ministry—Silent Unity—to pray for her. I prayed until I felt enveloped by great light and a sense of peace. Then I called a Unity Minister in Salt Lake City to visit her and continued to stay in that inner calm.

I waited several days and called the nurses' station at the hospital to inquire. I was told to wait a moment and then suddenly I heard my mother's voice. Not only was she able to come to the phone, but she was completely lucid. Generally it could take weeks for her to return to "reality." She had been poisoned with an overdose of lithium and had nearly died! She said to me, "Kathy, the most incredible thing has happened! I was in a dark tunnel feeling very frightened, when suddenly all this light came and enveloped me, and I know I was healed by prayer."

Prayer is our vehicle for discovering our oneness with God. The journey to wholeness (to sacred marriage) –to the palace of the sun—requires that we look honestly, openly, and with courage into ourselves, our feelings, our perceptions, our values, and our actions. It is a journey through our defenses, our temptations, and beyond so that we can awaken to the light of God.

Engaging Light

Prayer

Call upon the light of God to surround and enfold you. Ask for Divine illumination and know that you are one with all of the wisdom and understanding and knowledge of the Universe. Affirm: *"I am a radiant being of light."*

Meditation

Sit quietly in silence and relax. Imagine glorious light pouring into the top of your head through your crown chakra. Know that golden light is streaming through you revitalizing all of the cells and organs and systems of your body. You feel any remaining stress melting away in the light of God.

Physical Activity

Take time to play in the sun. Walk, run, ride a bicycle, or engage in some activity where you are aware of the sun's rays energizing you as you move.

Journaling

Have a written dialogue with your favorite Light Being: Jesus, Buddha, Mary, Krishna, Kwan Yin, an angel, animal, or other. Ask for wise counsel about how to be a greater light bearer in the world.

Stage Three
SACRED MARRIAGE
—From Separation to Union—

Experience

A steady "possession" of Divine awareness
in all states of consciousness

Challenge

Cultivation of non-dual consciousness

Danger

Temptation to transcendence—signing off from
earthly responsibility in the name of
"ultimate awareness"

Process

Unifying the opposites within
Embracing the Motherhood of God
Laboring for greater compassion and justice
in the world

Practice

Accepting and loving oneself in the present
moment
Exercises to reveal unconscious beliefs
Meditation on *The Motherhood of God*

In this third stage of *sacred marriage*—a knowledge of union with the Godhead in the deepest part of the self is made clearer and clearer, and an ever-steadier understanding of it is deepened progressively. This knowledge is nothing less than a new "birth"—the birth of the Divine person. No one has described this birth more accurately than Meister Eckhart:

"In this Divine birth I find that God and I are the same; I am what I was and what I shall remain, now and forever. I neither increase nor decrease, for in this birth I have become the motionless cause of all that moves. I have won back what has always been mine. Here, in my own soul, the greatest of all miracles has taken place—God has returned to God."

Andrew Harvey, *The Direct Path*, 57

Chapter 9

SACRED MARRIAGE

$\mathcal{M}$y healing experience with the Unity Minister in Texas struck a chord of longing in me. I longed for God, for love, for spiritual work, and for family. Feeling very alone, I packed up once again and my five year old son, Christopher, and I moved to Redding, California, in order to live near my sister Cheryl. Because she could not accommodate us in her small apartment, we moved in with her family friend Clark— the same man I had met in Salt Lake City at the basketball game where my heart was awakened.

Though roommates at first, Clark and I fell in love, married and had another son, Justin. It took my youngest son only five-and-a-half hours to enter the world, and he was beautiful and quite perfect, radiating a sweet tenderness. It was thrilling to have another child and to be able to share it this time. Clark adopted Chris, my oldest son, and I felt at last as though I had a complete family. Any residual fear of my former teacher now melted away altogether in this protective environment.

We were transferred throughout the northwest with Clark's work in the retail business, and it was there that my earlier invitation to compassion became a more specific call to ministry. We had joined the Unity church in Portland and one day when the minister walked down the aisle I had the thought, "I can do that!" The career counseling classes and personality tests confirmed that direction, and I began to pursue it. But then I went into three years of resistance, feeling unworthy. During that time we moved and finally, a minister in Everett, Washington helped me to apply for ministerial school. He was a kindred spirit who believed in my potential.

Clark left his job and our family of four moved from the Seattle area to Missouri, where I attended Unity School of Christianity, twenty-five miles southeast of Kansas City. I loved school and as I studied consciousness and metaphysics in a context of service, I felt like I had come home.

I was inspired by the lives of Myrtle and Charles Fillmore, the co-founders of Unity. They had started the Unity movement as a prayer circle that resulted from their personal healings. Influenced by the transcendentalists, they took the essence of truth from the various world religions and began a movement within the "New Thought" tradition that transcended all religious barriers. Their mystical vision combined with action in the world spoke to my heart.

During my time at Unity Village, I had two profound experiences that awakened a new level of conscious awareness and dramatically impacted my life. The first one was the result of an assignment given in my Metaphysics class. We were to write a paper describing who we believed Jesus to be. Was he an Avatar or Ascended Master who returned to awaken and save humankind? Was he an advanced soul who had traveled the spiritual path through many lives until he finally awakened? Was he just "one of the boys/girls," like you and me—who had a breakthrough and woke up?

We were to choose a viewpoint and then defend our position with the writings of Charles Fillmore. Actually, I found support for all three possibilities and intended to write the paper from that inclusive viewpoint. Something happened to me in the process though, and I found myself in the instructor's office in tears. I realized that I had held Jesus in such a transcendent place in my mind, that I had attracted the exact antithesis into my life in the form of a false spiritual teacher. Because I believed Jesus to be so advanced, there was no room in my philosophy to accept that Christ Consciousness might be possible for me in this lifetime. That was the moment of my breakthrough, and so I wrote from the third perspective: that "Jesus was just like you or me," as an affirmation of unlimited possibility. Since that time I have felt a greater sense of my own Divinity and have found it easier to "behold the Christ Presence" in others.

The second profound experience occurred when I was driving my six-year old son, Justin, to his daycare on my way to school very early one morning. While my son slept in the front seat I was practicing aloud a lecture that I was about to give on death and re-embodiment. At that moment a large deer jumped into the headlights and I had time only to brace myself for the impact. It catapulted us off the road into an embankment, which probably saved us from the traffic behind. Aside from a slight bump on the head, my son was okay. The deer, however, fell and got up, fell and got up again, about five times as it staggered all the way to my car window, where it looked directly into my eyes, collapsed one last time and died. Completely traumatized, I put my head down on the steering wheel and sobbed.

Several nights later, due to a strange set of circumstances involving a church dinner party that was progressing from one house to another, a shaman ended up at our house. She took me on a meditative dream journey to ask the deer why it died. It responded that it "died for my sins," and for the first time I understood what that meant and the meaning of sacrifice for another. I learned that the crucifixion is the death of the ego and the complete surrender of false thoughts and beliefs. I had been holding onto some old ideas and stories that I needed to release, and somehow the deer woke me up.

Later that week I met a Native American from the Deer Clan, and he told me that his people believed that when an animal sacrifices itself in such a way, its purpose is to give you its power. He said that the deer died to give me its power of "gentle strength."

On a second dream journey, the black widow spider came to me and since then it has become an important spirit guide, appearing in my dreams whenever I need warning. This has been a great and formidable totem during my years in ministry for it always identifies the trouble ahead of time so that I might be prepared.

The identity of "power" animals is supposed to be very private, but in cases when it may be educational for others, then it is not considered to be a frivolous ego-centered sharing. To realize that even the spirit of the fearful black widow can be a helpful compassionate being is a complete shattering of old perceptions.

This shamanic path opened up for me just as I was poised to "leap off the cliff" into ministry. I learned that the medicine person or shaman of indigenous cultures has traditionally been the main dreamer and healer for the entire community. He or she is versed in calling forth power. Many contemporary men and women practice shamanism and this is different than becoming a shaman. The term refers to those trained in traditional methods unique to indigenous cultures, or to westerners who have been apprenticed to native shamans and trained in their ways. A practitioner, on the other hand, is one who practices shamanism. Many people today have a shamanic type of calling. Like shamans, persons meant to work in the healing field are often wounded healers. They go through a crisis, die to an old personality, fight their way back to health and wholeness, and a more conscious life. They gain a certain quality that enables them to put others in touch with healing also.

Myrtle Fillmore, co-founder of Unity, had a type of shamanic calling. She was "chosen by the spirits," nearly dying from tuberculosis, but instead she was healed and then gained the ability to heal others. Charles Fillmore, her husband, followed suit for he was restored to health and wholeness after a childhood skating accident left him with a shrunken leg and infection causing impaired hearing and vision. But he was more of a dreamer who had many prophetic dreams and visions that guided him in the blossoming of the Unity work.

I thought of my mother and the many times she had returned from the world of madness to be a living example in my life, and I realized that she too had a shamanic calling—the life of a mystic who had carved her own unique path, without support or outer direction. She had been a willing sacrifice for me, like the deer, and all of the teachers and healers of my life, who walked before me on the path illuminating my way. Though I had never believed that Jesus had "died for my sins" in a sacrificial act, this entire idea was transformed into an understanding of his much more profound mission statement, "I came that you might have life and have it abundantly." We are each the living flame that can light the way for others on the quest for truth. My mother's radiance shone before me as I remembered that she taught me about the real gold to be found on a faith journey, and now I was about to discover that for myself. Gold, like faith, does not always come easily, and it certainly did not for me.

My marriage was shattered in the last quarter of ministerial school, and the divorce was final two months after my ordination. Devastated, my sons and I climbed into the U-haul truck, left the car and most of the furniture with their dad, and made the long drive to Tempe, Arizona where I had been hired to serve my first ministry.

In order to experience the true sacred marriage, we undergo a process of both release and integration. I had to let go of my old life in order to give birth to a new one centered in deeper service and surrender to the Will of God. This was a painful process, and for many months I was grieving the end of my marriage, while at the same time celebrating the birth of my new creative venture into ministry. As I began to lead others through a self discovery process, I stumbled onto my own path—the one I had been traveling from the beginning.

The Christian tradition has long held that there is a three-fold path to God: Illumination, Purgation, and Union. First we wake up to our higher potential, then we must purify ourselves, generally through some sort of privation, and finally, we experience our union with the Divine. Through Fall Programs in the church I began to work with this concept. Using more contemporary language, I called the framework:

"Preparation, Journey, and Return." It had essentially the same meaning as the more traditional one. I then added a mythic component, telling the congregation that we would be taking a three-month "heroic journey" of personal transformation. As heroes and heroines on our own quest for the true Self, we would focus on a particular stage each month. Each year for three years, these journeys evolved as we explored our spiritual power through various programs. Some incorporated Old Testament and Jungian archetypes, as well as a personal and a collective component. I discovered that whatever myth or story I selected, it would "play out" in the community. For example, if we took a three-month journey through the Old Testament, then during that time, the congregation would start to unconsciously act out those biblical stories and archetypes. One time when we reached the point in the story where the ten tribes of Israel divided, ten people in the church actually broke away in anger. I realized that I was onto something significant.

During the years that I worked with the three-fold path, I was trapped in a relationship. I had literally been struck by cupid's arrow, said to be a curse from the Gods since one becomes "sick with love." I had fallen in love at first sight with a man who was not entirely free. He lived with a woman who was very ill, and because the lightning bolt had struck both of us, we were condemned to three years of lunch dates. It was an ethereal realm of illusion, which I now know to be a complete "animus projection." He was a manifest vision of the masculine within me, and I became obsessed. One saving grace was a close male friend whom I have known since the beginning of my adventure into ministry. He and I have served as mirrors for one another and his counsel helps me to this day, not only in the church business arena, but in other dimensions of my life. His intuitive calls at just the right moments helped me escape my obsession.

I finally had to willfully force myself to let go and resist the temptation to ever see or call my fantasy lover again. This took place just as I had decided to do a Fall Program in the church using a four-fold path to God rather than the traditional three.

It was at this time that I stumbled upon Robert Johnson's book, *We*, in which he describes the Tristan and Isolde myth. To my amazement, it illumined my own story. Tristan is helping to escort Isolde by ship to a distant land where she is to wed a king. One night during their travels the two drink wine that contains a love potion meant for the bride and her future husband on the wedding night. These two are struck by the arrow and flee to an island where they stay for three years. They are starving and do not know it because they are lost in their enchantment. In the end, they have to part, but they exchange a ring, which proves to be their doom. It keeps them bound to one another, and to the old consciousness of "three," according to Johnson. He went on to say that if they had released one another completely, they would have progressed into the number four—that of wholeness, and a new world would have opened up for them.[1]

When I read this I was completely stunned, for I had let go, knowing that I could be lost in my obsession forever, while at the same time, declaring that we were going to take a journey in four stages in the church. We were moving from three to four in the ministry, just as I was in my own life. I had been unfolding my own process for all to see and participate in! I realized that my work of teaching and service was truly about the evolution of my own consciousness and that people could relate to the teachings because they described a path that had to be universally archetypal. Various mystics and spiritual leaders through the ages had pointed the way. And there is a certain place on the path where we wake up and become aware of our location. Once we discover the best framework or map for discerning the path, we are able to find a context in which to understand our life journey.

THE MOTHERHOOD OF GOD

It has been said that the three-fold path leaves out the feminine completely, and I found this to be true as I now immersed myself in the realm of four. At this station of awareness the Divine Mother became a constant presence.

The essence of the formless Divine Feminine reveals herself through the archetype of the Great Mother. She has both a good (creative) and terrible (destructive) side. Her various aspects have expressed themselves in the manifestation of goddess figures throughout the world. These always appear to be "outside," but are in fact an indirect experience of her inner archetypal images. In other words, we cannot perceive an archetype directly, for it is part of the contents of the unconscious, but we can see its reflection through the figures of gods and goddesses, and various symbols that appear in literature, art, religion, and every aspect of our lives.

Some of the feminine symbols are: moon, circle, egg, spiral, labyrinth, water, body, earth, container, cave, womb, serpent, tree of life, and others. Goddess figures emanating from The Great Mother include: Hathor, Isis, Inanna, Ishtar, Gaia, Athena, Aphrodite, Shekinah, Tara, Kali, Kwan Yin, Mary, Spider Woman, and others.

I realized that the Divine Mother first showed herself to me as the sacrificial deer, representing the Mother's gentle strength, and the Black Widow since Spider Woman has long been one of the powerful goddess figures. Next she was to reveal herself as Mary.

Through my continuing work with the number four and all of its implications, there have been four important teachers: the Divine Feminine, and three men who honor her: Matthew Fox, Jeremy Taylor, and Andrew Harvey. All three men have broken with traditional models in their own work and discovered their own unique expression of love in the world.

The first teacher, Matthew Fox, theologian and author, revived the Creation Spirituality tradition in the West, through emphasizing the world's mystical traditions in his prolific writing and at the school he founded in downtown Oakland, California. I had known of him when he was a Dominican

Priest undergoing his first silencing by the Vatican Council for his feminism and radical book *Original Blessing*. That of course, had captivated my interest which continued to grow after his excommunication from the Dominican Order.

But now I delved more fully into his work since he resurrected Meister Eckhart's idea that the mystical tradition can be named in four paths: Via Positiva, Negativa, Creativa, and Transformativa. Once again, my congregation and I journeyed together from the Fall Equinox to the Winter Solstice discovering the prize to be found in this powerful framework moving from awe, to mystery, to creative birth, and finally, compassionate transformation. Ultimately, after several years of deepening the process, it brought a visit from Matthew Fox to our church, and led me out of the Arizona ministry and to the Bay Area, where I would receive a Master's Degree from his school, "The University of Creation Spirituality," which was also affiliated with "Naropa Oakland."

Between Matt's visit and my eventual move I experienced a year of profound loss. It began in October, 1996, with the death of my mother, my beloved spiritual teacher and friend. During the four-month period when she was making her transition, I found myself in deep grief. One night I opened my mouth to pray aloud for help and heard myself saying a prayer to Mary. This actually shocked me since it was prayed "through me" and not from me. Though I had a love of Mother God, I generally had not focused on Mary. From that moment she began to manifest in my life in amazing ways. It began with one synchronistic experience after another. The night after the prayer someone saw her standing behind me, and I have had people tell me that occasionally ever since. Then I found a charm of the Madonna and child that had been blessed by the Pope in Italy and given to me as a gift from my former father-in-law. It was lost for years until that week when it suddenly appeared on my dresser! A friend in Florida sent a letter out of the blue, which included photos of Mary's image that could be seen in the glass windows of an office building in Tampa. The chain of events continued to unfold.

On my final visit with my mother in Salt Lake City prior to her death, I told her of the Mary experiences and her comment to me was, "Oh, Mary is a most important key!" To this day I wish I could question her further about her personal experience of that revelation.

Mary was present for me through my mother's death and for the entire year of change and transition concluding with my leaving the church and moving to Northern California. My oldest son Chris moved with me, but my youngest son, Justin, at age fourteen, went to live with his Dad in North Dakota for his own rite of passage. I lost my mother, and my youngest son for the time being, but the Divine Mother came to comfort me as daughter and parent. I could feel her weeping with me, and to this day I am healed by her love and compassion.

Mary's guidance actually provided the impetus for me to enroll in the program at the University of Creation Spirituality in Oakland, and ultimately to make the move one year after my mom's passing. While still in grief I had been elected to a national position on the Executive Committee of the Association of Unity Churches. I was wrestling with a dilemma that I faced in regard to the pursuit of positional power or spiritual power. My heart was drawn to Matthew Fox's school which honored the feminine in the four paths, while my head screamed at me that I could make a difference helping to set policy for the Unity Movement.

One day I went to lunch with a Minister friend. In the midst of our conversation she stopped in amazement and said, "Kathy, last night I had a visit from Mary. She told me she has a message for you and to give it to you if you said the words to me that you just spoke!" I have no idea today what they were, but the message she then gave me was this:

"Mary said to tell you that you are in a tractor beam. All you can do is surrender and go with it and everything is going to unfold beautifully."

I was speechless! It may not sound very dramatic, but the words "tractor beam" resonated within me and my eyes burned with tears. It was a very unique expression that my mother had often used to describe the compelling cosmic forces that urge us forward on our path. This was not referring to the beam of a farm tractor, but rather, the gravitational force field of a space station pulling one in like a magnet. The moment I heard the message I knew it was deeply personal and that I was to resign from positional power and continue my journey following my heart into a deeper awareness of God.

That is exactly what the Divine Mother calls us to. She is urging us to embrace the sacred feminine by developing the child, the mystic, and the prophet in ourselves and our world. We must nurture the world's children for they are the future, as well as the "inner child," for it teaches us to play and to laugh at ourselves. We must awaken the mystic, the compassionate one who realizes our oneness and brings us the wisdom that we need. And we are invited to invoke the Prophet, the one who sees and is willing to speak out against injustice in the name of the Mother for the greater good of all.

Chapter 10

MARRYING SELF

Marriage is a fine institution
but I'm not ready for an institution yet.

Mae West

*M*arriage is the mystical and sacred blending of two different and seemingly opposite elements. Traditionally we think of marriage as an outward joining of two people. In fact during the marriage ceremony, the energies of the two partners are blended into one energy. Although each of the individuals retains uniqueness as well, there is also a new unified being—one in love.

Sacred Marriage refers to an inner transformation. It describes the integration of our personality and soul, our shadow and our authentic self, our masculine and feminine sides. Actually it is not just an integration, but an alchemical fusing together of all the opposites that we hold in our minds. The sacred marriage is also a metaphor for our wholeness.

Whether we are married in the outer world or not, the inner marriage is available to each one of us as we come to know that we are both human and Divine, and that we can love ourselves exactly as we are—embracing all of ourselves— darkness and light—without judgment.

In this station of the path we move from separation to union.

We begin to have a steady possession of Divine awareness that is present in all that we do. We truly know that we are one with God and with all life.

Ever since I can remember, I have longed for a soul mate. It fueled a lifelong search, which included two marriages and took place in the outer world at first for many years. Some are blessed to find such a partner and even then the spiritual path is ultimately a very personal one. We may have allies, even in the form of a soul mate to help us, but we still experience the Divine marriage within our *own* souls. Each one of us, married or single, has the potential for the sacred marriage in which we open our hearts in a union with the Divine self.

I love what children have to say when asked about marriage:

Eric, age 6 said, "Marriage is when you get to keep your girl and don't have to give her back to her parents!"

When asked how a person decides whom to marry, Kally, age 9 said, "You flip a nickel, and heads mean you stay with him and tails mean you try the next one."

Carolyn, age 8 said, "My mother says to look for a man who is kind...that's what I'll do...I'll find somebody who's kinda tall and handsome."[1]

Through the preceding chapters we have looked at some of the obstacles encountered along the way to sacred marriage: the temptations of the ego, the childhood issues that arise for us, the need to release fears, negative behaviors, and false beliefs.

Does it mean that we must become free of all negativity before this inner marriage can occur? The answer is no—we still live in the earth plane and yet it is possible to experience heaven on earth. Divine Marriage is not strictly a question of "getting rid of" or "releasing." Another way to perceive it is "unifying" the opposites within us.

Consciousness in this world is polarized into pairs of opposites, such as: good/bad, right/wrong, pain/ pleasure, win/lose, and many more. It is possible to find the underlying unity inherent in all the pairs of opposites within us so that we may experience sacred marriage.

Carl Jung wrote extensively about the unification of opposites. He said, "Nothing can exist without its opposite; the two were one in the beginning and will be one again in the end. Therefore, the perfected sage liberates himself from the opposites."[2]

A wedding is often symbolic of this unification, and Jesus tells this profound story about a wedding feast:

> The Kingdom of Heaven may be compared to a king who gave a marriage feast for his son, and sent his servants to call those who were invited to the marriage feast; but they would not come.
>
> Again, he sent other servants saying, "Tell those who are invited, behold, I have made ready my dinner, my oxen and my fat calves are killed, and everything is ready; come to the marriage feast." But they made light of it and went off, one to his farm, another to his business, while the rest seized his servants, treated them shamefully and killed them. The king was angry, and he sent his troops and destroyed those murderers and burned their city. Then he said to his servants, "The wedding is ready, but those invited were not worthy. Go therefore to the thoroughfares, and invite to the marriage feast as many as you find." And those servants went out into the streets and gathered all whom they found, both bad and good; so the wedding hall was filled with guests.
>
> But when the king came in to look at the guests, he saw there a man who had no wedding garment; and he said to him, "Friend, how did you get in here without a wedding garment?" And he was speechless.
>
> Then the king said to the attendants, "bind him hand and foot, and cast him into the outer darkness; there men will weep and gnash their teeth." For many are called, but few are chosen.[3]

The wedding feast is the Kingdom/Queendom of Heaven that each one of us is invited to as heirs. The King (The Divine Self) sends servants or inner promptings to invite us. But we often make light of it by being too busy or even killing the ideas in our own consciousness.

Now the king sends troops that destroy the murderers and burn the city. The Self will persist in overwhelming us with the inner calling until our old complacency and sense of separation is destroyed. The Divine Self will send the message into the thoroughfares, into all aspects of our being and gather us into the wedding hall, the inner temple.

But the king discovers one without a wedding garment and binds him and casts him into outer darkness. Those parts of ourselves that are unwilling to be prepared for the wedding remain in the darkness of the unconscious. Many are called, but few are chosen. We are all given the opportunity to enter into the Kingdom/Queendom of God—the enlightened state of consciousness—but few of us choose to experience the sacred marriage and then to complete the journey.

Some of us are confused about the idea of marriage. A little boy attended his first wedding. After the service his cousin asked him, "How many women can a man marry?" "Sixteen," the boy responded. His cousin was amazed that he had an answer so quickly. "How do you know that?" "Easy," the little boy said. "All you have to do is add it up like the bishop said, '4 better, 4 worse, 4 richer, 4 poorer.'"[4]

One of the most memorable weddings I ever performed still reminds me about the power of love to transcend opposites and unite what is meant to be together. In the month of January sometime in the early 90's a woman and her mother met with me in my church office in Tempe, Arizona, where I was serving at the time. The woman, Sara, wanted me to perform her wedding in the coming summer. She explained to me that she had met her husband in England during a two week vacation there. Her husband-to-be was still in England but would be coming for the August ceremony. I felt reluctant since they had only known each other two weeks, but then she and her mother shared her amazing story. She had planned a trip to England with friends and had been saving money to go. She lived at home with her mother who was somewhat possessive and had always disapproved of Sara's boyfriends.

One night Sara said to her mother, "Maybe I should not go. I could just use the money to pay off my bills." Sara's mother related to me that in that moment she thought: "If she does not go she will not meet him." But she said nothing and allowed her daughter to make her decision without interference.

Sara decided to take the trip and the moment she stepped off the plane in London she felt like she was home. She and her friends stayed with people they knew who lived above an upscale pub. The first night their English friends threw a party for them in the pub to celebrate their arrival. Sara walked downstairs, glanced down a row of tables, and saw "him" sitting there. She was struck by the lightning bolt. She then spent the rest of the evening trying to avoid him while he attempted to pursue her. When he finally was able to connect with her, he introduced himself as Tom and explained that cupid's arrow had found him as well. It was love at first sight for both of them. They spent every moment together over the next few weeks while Sara was in England. By the time she returned to the states they were making wedding plans.

The interesting part of the story was that Sara's mother, always disapproving of the men in her life, was ecstatic about the match, even though it meant that her daughter would be moving away to England.

When Tom arrived in August the wedding did take place. I was amazed, for the couple was quite the opposite of what is generally portrayed in the great "love at first sight" romances. She weighed probably over 250 pounds and was not in the least physically attractive. He was thin as a rail with tattoos on most of his exposed skin, except his face. And in addition, he had a speech impediment—a slight stutter.

I mixed up their rings in the ceremony since she was the larger of the two. But what I shall never forget, what still brings tears to my eyes, was the power of the love between them. I felt it as a physical force as I performed their ceremony and it remains as present for me today as it was then.

That wedding has always been a powerful reminder of the fact that love can unite the most unlikely pair of opposites. It transcends time, space, and all outer appearances and unites what is meant to be together.

In order to open ourselves to sacred marriage we must unify the opposites we hold in our minds and come to know our oneness with everything. In the Bhagavad Gita, the primary scripture of Hinduism, Krishna speaks of the unification of opposites to Arjuna. He says, "You must be free from the pairs of opposites. Poise your mind in tranquility."[5]

In Buddhism, the Buddha advocated the middle path, walking between the pairs of opposites, to reach enlightenment.

In the Gnostic text, *The Gospel according to Thomas,* Jesus said, "When you make the two one, and when you make the inner as the outer and the outer as the inner and the above as the below, and when you make the male and the female into a single one, so that the male will not be male and the female not be female…then shall you enter the kingdom."[6]

This stunningly profound statement by Jesus summarizes the sacred marriage. When we see beyond separation and duality to the underlying unity that is love, we come to know that it is, in fact, a great wedding feast to which we are all invited.

Marrying Self

Prayer

Call upon the Presence and Power of the Divine Mother to be with you and to reveal your true nature. Ask that your endeavors to integrate all of the aspects of your self, be blessed. Affirm: "*God and I are one.*"

Meditation

Sit quietly and relax. Breathe deeply and imagine relaxing all of the muscles of the body, beginning with the feet and working your way up. Then sweep any remaining tension from your head all the way down through your feet and into the earth, where it is transformed. When relaxed ask the question, "*Who am I?*"

Physical Activity

Cultivate the "witness" throughout the day. This is the Divine self, who observes us in our dance of polarity. Observe yourself from this perspective, as you engage in daily exercise or walking. Send love just as you are.

Journaling

Note any dreams and also responses to the previous question asked above, "*Who am I?*" What images or thoughts arose in response?

Chapter 11

MARRYING COMMUNITY

$\mathcal{P}$eople come together in community at weddings. One of my great community experiences took place at a wedding I performed in Arizona. It was a home wedding in a lovely housing development situated on a lake. We were in the backyard, and I was in the corner of the yard facing the house with my back to the lake. The bride and groom and their guests faced me and had a beautiful view of the lake behind me.

I was coming to the part of the ceremony where I was about to ask the crowd to join together in greater community in a spirit of love to bless this couple as I was to pronounce them husband and wife.

Behind me in the lake there was a subtle crackling noise that began to increase in intensity. I soon realized that it was the sound of ducks. As I approached the zenith of the ceremony, their voices grew insistently loud. The people were beginning to react. Finally just as I was to invoke the group blessing—the ducks arrived—an entire community of them pulled up behind me, all quacking at the top of their lungs. It was a fabulous moment! We were all overcome with the wondrous humor of it all and the greater community of which we are an integral part.

> Community means different things to different people. To some it is a safe haven where survival is assured. To others it is a place of emotional support where there is deep sharing and bonding with close friends. Some see community as an intense crucible for personal growth. For others, it is primarily a place to pioneer their dreams.

> ...It's true—we are embedded in communities, circles within circles of communities, both, small and large, focused and abstract, strangers and loved ones. Holding up the ideal of unity, we strive to break down the walls which separate us from others—not only other nations and peoples, but other species and the natural world.[1]

Catholic Priest, Richard Rohr said, "*Everything belongs* has become my motto and mantra. *Everything belongs.* By keeping an open mind and spirit, we reach out to the stranger and to all those who are different from us."[2]

In this stage of sacred marriage we take the theme of "marrying self" through unifying the opposites within us, a step further. Unifying opposites continues to apply because always in community we are dealing with ourselves and with others. We are in agreement or disagreement. And just as in a marriage, where we have to accept the dark and the light through the power of love, so also is it true in community.

Ram Dass tells how he dealt with that sense of frustration when in disagreement:

> There was a time when my aggravation with the system focused on the Secretary of Defense. I'm sure he was no worse than many others, but there was something about his cold arrogance and apparent lack of wisdom that infuriated me. So I got a picture of him and placed it on my prayer table with all my spiritual heroes. Then, each morning when I lit my incense and honored the beings represented on the prayer table, I'd feel waves of love and appreciation toward my guru, Buddha, Christ, and the others. I'd wish them each good morning with such tenderness. Then I'd come to the Secretary's picture, and I'd feel my heart constrict, and I'd hear the coldness in my voice as I said, "Good morning, (adding his name)." Each morning I'd see what a long way I still had to go.

> But wasn't he just another face of God? Couldn't I oppose his actions and still keep my heart open to him? Wouldn't it be harder for him to become free from the role he was obviously trapped in if I, with my mind, just kept reinforcing the traps by identifying him with his acts?[3]

The Indian poet Kabir said …"Do what you do to another person, but never put them out of your heart." It's a tall order. But what else is there to do?[4]

Marrying community means unifying the opposites within ourselves and the outer world. It also means we no longer have to do it alone. We join with others in shared mission using our gifts and talents in order to be connected and to serve through the power of love.

I consider churches I have served, for example. Those involved are all in a specific spiritual community. The church is a circle within the larger circle of the Unity movement. And the movement is a circle within countless others of light and love and truth in the world. And this applies to all of us in whatever spiritual community of which we are a part.

Each of us enters at a different place coming from various backgrounds, at unique stages in our growth. Some of us may have been aware of our spiritual journey for many years. Others are new to the path. Things may be wonderful for some of us now, while others may have sought community because they are in pain.

The main reason people attend church or find any spiritual community is for connecting with others and for spiritual growth. Whenever people form a group there is a tendency for a greater sense of security and belonging, and also an enhanced potential for pain. All communities become healthier when there is a creative context for their joys and their troubles.

For example, it helps to realize that an organized community, whether it is a church or a business organization or a country, is a living, evolving organism. Like an individual, it goes through periods of grief and sadness and challenging times, but also growth and prosperity and experiences of profound Divine love.

Some of us can look back on our own lives and see that there were years of dark ordeals, and there have also been powerful periods of joy and love. The same is true of a larger collective. Just as individuals are born anew, so too are communities, especially when there is a guiding principle of love to live by.

The description of geese is a wonderful model for us:

> We are like geese. In the fall or spring, when you see geese heading south for the winter, flying along in "v" formation, you might be interested in what scientists have discovered about why they fly that way.
>
> As each bird flaps its wings, it creates an uplift for the bird immediately following. By flying in "v" formation, the whole flock adds at least 71% greater flying range than if each bird flew on its own.
>
> People who share a common direction and sense of community can get where they are going more quickly and easily, because they are traveling on the thrust of one another.
>
> When a goose falls out of formation, it suddenly feels

the drag and resistance of trying to go it alone—and quickly gets back into formation to take advantage of the lifting power of the bird in front.

If we have as much sense as a goose, we will stay in formation with those people who are headed the same way we are.

When the head goose gets tired, it rotates back in the wing and another goose flies point.

It is sensible to take turns doing demanding jobs, whether with people or with geese flying south.

Geese honk from behind to encourage those up front to keep up their speed. What messages do we give when we honk from behind?

Finally, and this is important, when a goose gets sick or is wounded by gunshot, and falls out of formation, two other geese fall out with that goose and follow it down to lend help and protection. They stay with the fallen goose until it is able to fly or until it dies; and only then do they launch out on their own, or with another formation to catch up with their group.

If we have the sense of a goose, we will stand by each other like that.[5]

Marrying community means that our own mission or purpose intersects with that of the group. Each of us has three aspects of mission in life:

1) An inner mission in which our task is to seek personal spiritual growth by awakening the Christ presence within.

2) A shared mission in which we join together with others to make this world a better place.

3) A unique mission in which we use our own unique gifts and talents in service for the highest good.[6]

Certainly these intersect in our various communities, but especially in spiritual community. The first one, an inner mission in which we seek personal spiritual growth by awakening the Christ Presence within, is marrying self, as discussed in *Chapter 9*. This is unifying the opposites within.

The second, a shared mission where we join together with others to make this world a better place, is marrying community. Though it is a very personal process to become enlightened, it is also helpful to find community where we can support one another in our own growth and spiritual development. We make the world a better place as we work through challenges in the group and unify the opposites within our communities in an environment of love.

The third, a specific shared mission is marrying creation, discussed in chapter 10 in the context of both saving and savoring the world. In addition to that idea, we are called to use our own special gifts in making a difference. Our true spiritual gifts and unique talents are discovered by following inner guidance and doing what we most love to do. There are many arenas where people can serve according to their gifts and also their passions. Certainly there is much to be done in this world with a wide spectrum of skills needed. When we act in service to God, to love, and to the community, we find our creative fulfillment, but it is essential that we take action.

Sometimes in the spiritual journey we need personal healing and have no energy for further involvement. However, there is a point reached when we can look beyond our own personal needs and include the community. We begin to focus on the word *responsibility*—the ability to respond— and we ask questions. What is my responsibility in the greater community? How might I serve God in a collective environment? There are always different levels of involvement—from very minimal to deeply committed. Each of us must follow the dictates of our own heart in regard to the actions we take.

When we join together in a particular shared mission to transform the world, that is in fact exactly what happens—we make the world a better place. Margaret Mead said, "Never underestimate the power of a small group to change the world. Indeed it is the only thing that ever has."

When unconditional loving service becomes a way of life and we activate these three aspects of mission, we intersect with the world's needs and become an agent of change in the global community. This is, in fact, marrying community. We marry our spiritual awakening with community involvement and our own unique gifts.

There is a story called "The Rabbi's Gift" that addresses the way we become a change agent:

> There was once a monastery that had fallen upon hard times. Once a great order, it had become decimated to the extent that there were only five monks left: the abbot and four others, all over 70 in age. Clearly it was a dying order.
>
> In the deep woods surrounding the monastery there was a little hut that a rabbi from a nearby town occasionally used for a hermitage. The time came for the rabbi and the abbot to meet there for one of their rare visits. They commiserated about the fact that the spirit had gone out of the people. They wept together and read and spoke of deep things. The time came when the abbot had to leave. They embraced and the abbot asked, "Have you no advice to give me?"
>
> "No, I am sorry," the rabbi responded, "I have no advice to give. The only thing I can tell you is that the Messiah is one of you."
>
> When the abbot returned to the monastery, his fellow monks gathered around him to ask, "Well, what did the rabbi say?"
>
> "He couldn't help," the abbot answered. "The only thing he did say was that the Messiah is one of us."
>
> In the days and weeks that followed the old monks pondered this and wondered whether it was true. Do you

suppose he meant the abbot? He has been our leader for so long. On the other hand, he might have meant Brother Thomas. Everyone knows he is a man of light. Certainly he could not have meant Brother John. He is so cranky, but then he is also very wise. Brother Phillip is so passive and weak. But then he always speaks so kindly of everyone. Maybe he is the Messiah. Of course the rabbi didn't mean me. He couldn't possibly have meant me.

As they contemplated in this manner, the old monks began to treat each other and themselves with extraordinary respect on the off-chance that one of them might be the Messiah. Then it happened that some of the younger men who came to visit the monastery began to join and once again it became a vibrant center of light and spirituality in the realm.[7]

May each of us do our part to create community that radiates light and loving kindness throughout the land.

Marrying Community

Prayer

Pray for someone you disagree with, attempting to see him or her as a being of light and love. Pray for your spiritual community if you have one and also for the global community. Affirm: *"My relationships are harmonious and fulfilling."*

Meditation

Sit quietly and relax your mind and body. Reflect on a community that you are part of, considering its strengths and challenges. Now see the community as part of you and not separate. Know that the community *is* you. Ask yourself, how can I be a greater force for love and how can I better use my talents in this community?

Physical Activity

Go hiking or take a walk with a friend or a small group of people and have an intention to experience yourself as part of a greater whole in community with others.

Journaling

Continue to record your dreams. Write your response to the question, "With love as my Guide and service as my path, what is my own specific mission in the world?"

Chapter 12

MARRYING CREATION

Every morning I awaken torn between the desire to save
the world and the inclination to savor it.[1]

E.B. White

*T*his statement is at the heart of our sacred marriage to
all of creation—uniting our desire to savor the world with the
desire to save it. It is the in-breath—breathing in the blessing
that we receive, and the out-breath—breathing out the blessing that we are.

We are all one, woven together in the great web of life,
and when we know that, we are awestruck with an incredible
gratitude for the wonder of life. Then we are also filled with
the pain of the world and a desire to serve out of a deepened
compassion.

In India this awakening or marriage is often called "seeing the Jeweled Net of Indra." This is the net of creation where in each intersection of the net there is a reflective jewel of an individual woven together with and reflecting all of the other strands of existence.[2]

With our deepening connection to the natural world we want to retreat into our bliss and thankfulness, spending time in prayer or meditation or simply play. On the other hand, we want to do something to help, to serve the greater good.

In this third stage of the path, Sacred Marriage, Andrew Harvey says that the main challenge is the temptation to transcendence. In its extreme form, this is when an enlightened being stays in bliss consciousness—signing off from earthly responsibility.

Further down on the continuum it can be a selfish desire to savor creation. We want to meditate, go to workshops, pray, play, and work solely on ourselves. We do not allow gratitude to motivate us to action, but instead we are caught up in longing for the Divine at the expense of the world.

There is a story told of St. John of the Cross, alone in his room in profound prayer. He experienced a rapturous vision of Mary. At the same moment he heard a beggar rattling at his door for alms. He wrenched himself away and saw to the beggar's needs. When he returned, the vision returned again, saying that at the very moment he had heard the door rattle on its hinges, his soul had hung in perilous balance. Had he not gone to the beggar's aid, she could never have appeared to him again.[3]

A milder form of the same dilemma occurred for me recently. There was an ad that appeared on the bulletin board in my ministry for an evening presentation about Mary at another local church. There was going to be a discussion of the recent Mary sightings and an overview of Mary in the world. I was very interested in this since Mary is important to me as a loving expression of the Divine Mother. I wanted to attend this event and I had to choose—go hear about Mary or go to a movie with my nineteen year old son. I went to the movie. It was not the kind of wrestling that St. John of the Cross had to experience but there was a similar element. Will I pursue my own connection with the Mother, or will I be engaged with my son as mother? And ironically, through that engagement in the world we find our connection anyway. I had a great time with Justin at the movie—one of those joyful moments in time.

I also had a memorable incident occur while I was writing this chapter. I was at the exact point that I just mentioned—St. John's choice between Mary or the beggar at the door—and my doorbell rang! I opened the door and there was a young teenage girl selling magazines for her career path. I was preoccupied with my book and I said no. I closed the door, went upstairs, and then it struck me. Suddenly I felt desperate to help her. Oh no, I failed the test! I said no to the person at the door and Mary will never speak to me again! So I stepped outside and could not see the girl anywhere. I walked down the steps into the front yard looking for her and scraped my leg against the brick retaining wall. Now I had a wound from the experience! Finally as I was about to give up I saw her down the street, so I retrieved my keys and climbed into my car. When I turned the ignition on a CD was playing and the song was *Amazing Grace*. I was saved!

I drove up to the young woman and said, "I've changed my mind." I did not tell her I was trying to "redeem myself." I was inwardly laughing for I do not believe that Father/Mother God withholds anything. We only have to ask, for God's generosity is never-ending. As I bought the magazine I inquired what career path she was on that this purchase was supporting. She said she wanted to be a nurse. Her parting words to me were, "God bless you!"

I did have to choose between a magazine for one of my sons or for myself, and I bought one for me. I determined a little self care was in order; after all, I was bleeding!

Andrew Harvey says that when one overcomes the temptation to transcendence—the temptation to focus only on our own bliss and forget the world, we can then become a bodhisattva. Those taking the Bodhisattva vows in Mahayana Buddhism pledge themselves to return to this world of pain and constriction forever until every sentient creature is finally liberated. This is laboring "to birth transformation in all conditions of worldly life."[4]

Harvey says that in our sacred marriage with our own Divine nature and all of creation, we must "embrace the

Motherhood of God that created the creation and sustains it with infinite love…and tireless action…freed by transcendent wisdom, we can dive…into the heart of immanence—(into the world) and work there (in dedicated love)."[5]

It is so important that we not only "save the world" but that we take time to "savor it" by appreciating all that we have and being thankful for our blessings, for the great wedding banquet of creation.

> The Creator God is a gracious, an abundant, and a generous host/hostess. She has spread out for our delight a banquet that was twenty billion years in the making. A banquet of rivers and lakes, of rain and of sunshine, of rich earth and of amazing flowers, of handsome trees and of dancing fishes, of contemplative animals and of whistling winds, of dry and wet seasons, of cold and hot climates. But it is a banquet that works, this banquet we call creation, the human planet. It works for our benefit if we behave toward it as reverent guests. God has declared that this banquet is 'very good' and so are we, blessings ourselves, invited to the banquet.[6]

When we savor creation we know that we are blessed, and as we serve it through loving action, we know that we are a blessing. I believe that one of the best ways that we can marry these two powerful forces of a wondrous, reflective gratitude, with an active mission of service—is to begin simply by saying, "Thank you."

The words "thanksgiving" and "praise" can be used inter-changeably for they mean virtually the same thing. It is true also that we increase whatever we praise. ". . . All there is responds to a word of praise. God responds. We respond. Everything responds. The whole world sparkles, quivers, comes alive. Things vibrate and are quickened. We vibrate and are quickened. Heaven and earth are in tune with us, and we are in tune with them. When we give praise, everything wants to give in return."[7]

We can begin simply by praising and saying "thank you" to ourselves, our minds, our bodies, to others for all that they do, to our loved ones, and to strangers who help us in small ways. And if our loved ones have crossed over to the other side, we can still send our thanks. No one ever passes beyond the power of prayer or the realm of Spirit. The expression of gratitude has the power to bless the world and beyond.

One of the most memorable family Thanksgiving dinners I ever had was one where my family and I decided to take turns around the dinner table and tell everyone what we appreciated about them and what we were grateful for. We were all in tears by the time it was complete because it was so moving to experience others being appreciated and to receive that kind of praise as well. It raised the question, "Why should we wait for Thanksgiving to share our gratitude with loved ones?" When we tune into gratitude on a regular basis, we come to see the Divine in everything and to know our oneness, and this is the Sacred Marriage. We come to understand the great generosity of creation.

> We are part of a magnificent universe that is blessing us all of the time. Without even talking about all of the trillions of stars and galaxies we can simply consider the sun. Each second it transforms four million tons of itself into light. Each second a huge chunk of it vanishes into radiant energy that soars away in all directions. The sun is sacrificing itself that we might have life. Where have we heard that before? It is giving itself over to become energy that we, with every meal, partake of. For four million years humans have been feasting on the sun's energy stored in wheat or animals as each day the sun dies and is reborn as the vitality of earth.

> The sun's bestowal of energy is an impulse pervading the universe. In the human heart it is felt as the urge to devote one's life to the well being of the larger community. Human love and generosity are possible only because at the center of the solar system a magnificent stellar generosity pours forth free energy day and night without stop and without complaint and without hesitation. This is the way of the universe—the way of life.

> We are living beings within an evolving galactic process. And the universe is being born in us. Scientists and mystics know that because the universe is holographic, like the net of Indra, each of us is at the center of creation. Each of us has a magnificent opportunity to express this life which the sun makes possible.[8]

We are blessed and we are a blessing. It is the in-breath and the out-breath of life, Mother/Father God. So take time to savor the wonders of this world and also to save it—and begin by feeling grateful and saying "thank you."

Marrying Creation

Prayer

Call upon the Divine Mother of all life to bless creation, to bless the environment of this beautiful planet, to bless all sentient beings everywhere. Affirm: *"Thank you Goddess!"*

Meditation

Sit in the Silence and send love and light throughout the planet. Begin by imagining light all around you, then extend it to others in the room, in the city, the state, the country, and the earth. Then extend yourself into space, sending love and light into its vastness. Then look back at the earth, and send it to all beings everywhere. Bring yourself back into your body by returning the way you came.

Physical Activity

Take a gratitude walk, silently or aloud praising and thanking the Divine Mother, people, animals, trees, flowers, and all of the wonders that you pass.

Journaling

List all of the blessings you can think of in a spirit of complete gratitude.

Stage Four
BIRTHING
—From Conception to Transformation—

Experience

Transformation into a mystic revolutionary and
a co-creator of a new sacred reality

Challenge

Suffering through the birth canal and the
heartbreak of pure love for all beings

Danger

The provocation of dislike, rage and even
hatred in others
Trying to control rather than surrendering

Process

Refining the integration of spirit, soul, and body
Inner and outer transformation
Opening to the needs and pains of others

Practice

Continued prayer and meditation
Aspiring to be a humble servant of God
Living in the joy of birthing divine truth and
justice

"Birthing" is about being a mystic revolutionary and a co-creator in and with God of a new integral sacred reality... You are to be a living, ardent tool with which the Supreme artist works, one of the instruments of His Self-manifestation—the perpetual process by which His reality is birthed into concrete expression.

The rewards of "birthing" are "birthing" itself—knowing that through divine grace you are becoming more and more of an instrument of divine love and justice....

Andrew Harvey, *The Direct Path* (62-63)

Jesus said: "You shall love the Lord your God with all your heart, and with all your soul, and with all your strength, and with all your mind; and your neighbor as yourself."

Luke 10: 26-27

As each one of us puts these words into action, we have the power to birth a new world!

Chapter 13

BIRTHING

$\mathcal{W}$e are all called to give birth to the Divine. We are paradoxically giving birth and being born at the same time. The path is a spiral and so we can sometimes experience the stages of it simultaneously. I gave birth to my sons, for example, during an overall time of "Engagement" and "Sacred Marriage." They came in a phase of my life when I was engaging a deeper intention to find God and marry the opposites within to discover my authentic self.

The process of "Birthing" permeates everything. Meister Eckhart said, "God is creating the entire universe fully and totally in this present now."[1] There is also a specific season for birthing on the spiritual path. After we have united some of the opposite polarities within us we are then ready to give birth to a new identity, a transformed consciousness and the resulting creative expression.

Ready for a new identity and once again stepping out on faith, I resigned from my church in Tempe, Arizona and my position on the Executive Committee of the Association of Unity Churches. I moved to Northern California, and my first new "baby" at this time was a Master's Degree from the University of Creation Spirituality (Naropa West). It was there I met my second male guide, Jeremy Taylor, world-renowned dream worker and author. He was the chair of my Master's Thesis, and he encouraged me to write a book. He has since taught me, what I believe, is the world's most effective method of dream interpretation, and helped me to become certified as a Dream Worker in his "Taylor" method. It was through his work with my own dreams that I was guided to my next ministry at Unity Temple of Santa Cruz not only once, but a second time as well. His understanding of symbols and mythic images hearkened back to my early childhood education in magical perceptions. He gave me essential puzzle pieces that illumined many aspects of my life. I am eternally grateful to him for his friendship, his mentoring, his hours of personal counsel, and for the Projective Dream Work Certification Program in which he bestowed his mantle of wisdom.

My dreams led me to Unity Temple of Santa Cruz in the summer of 1998 as a Temporary Minister. I was able to serve there while simultaneously completing my Master's degree. It was a one-year assignment to consult and assist in healing the church conflict. We were able to come to a fairly peaceful solution. However, I chose to leave at the year's end in order to pursue a Unity Workshop Ministry in Southern California and a much needed rest.

I moved to that specific location in order to be with a man who had come into my life. The relationship caused severe labor pains as I strove to give birth to a whole self, complete with a greater awareness of my shadow side. After a year together, we spent six months in Jungian analysis in an effort to exit the relationship consciously. I was able to see the different aspects of my psyche and take responsibility for my part in the dynamic. At the same time we could see that the "oil and water" nature of the relationship would never work.

This phase of my life was the midlife passage of "Psyche's Journey to the Underworld." We are always "tricked" into the underworld for we would not go there willingly. It is the dark realm of the unconscious waiting for illumination when we dare to open the door.

The darkness actually continued for me as I returned to Northern California alone. I found a house in Santa Cruz, where I had longed to return. But I commuted over treacherous Highway 17 an hour each way to the Palo Alto Unity Church for the next fourteen months. I could not escape my black mood, and the church was not a fit for me other than to shine more light on aspects of my unconscious. There were many wonderful people, but I was plagued by the loss of a relationship and also my personal power. I was working as an Associate Minister and did not have the usual free reign I needed for my particular management style. I was also deeply troubled by a prophetic dream that I had in January of 2001 about September 11th. It haunted me for months before the disastrous event. I was emotionally distressed and physically ill through most of that year.

In the dream, I am in a tall skyscraper and through the window I can see a second skyscraper just across from me. Suddenly I am looking through a portal and can see the top of both buildings. The one I am in has a spire, and I think to myself that it reminds me of the Empire State Building (though I do not make the connection with the Twin Towers). On the roof of the building next to mine I see that there is a delivery semi-truck with a foreign driver in it. I realize with horror that the man is crazy and is going to attempt a flying leap onto the top of my building. I am wondering how I can stop him.

I go down to the ground floor of the building and discover a circular interior courtyard. It is filled with women. I see a minister that I recognize sitting on a couch with her head in her grandmother's lap. I acknowledge how nurturing that seems. Another young woman comes up to me and says, "I will be your grandmother. Do you want me to be your grandmother?" I respond sharply, "No! I do not want you to be my grandmother."

Then I walk outside the building and look up to discover that the foreign driver has made his delivery and the truck is impaled on the spire. I am terror stricken, and I say to myself, "How will I ever get it down? I am going to have to find a crane!"

I invited dream groups to help analyze this dream, and in the Spring of 2001, Jeremy Taylor spent an hour assisting me with the interpretation. I remember him asking, "What is the truck delivering?" and I responded, "Food, it is bringing food." At the end of his projected interpretation he said, "This is beyond personal. It is very archetypal and collective, relating to all of us, like a Native American 'big dream' and the gods are watching this one."

Because I had been recently employed in a church with a large spire, I believed it related to my work. However, I could not overcome the feeling of death all around me and a sense of overwhelming anxiety, and I became increasingly depressed.

At last, several months after the catastrophe, I felt a new birth occurring within me, and I announced in November that I was going to find another church. Two weeks later Unity Temple of Santa Cruz became available. Once again the church was in another transition, and I was the logical minister to step in. Conveniently I was already living there and was happy to return. It was an amazing full circle journey, and this time I ventured in with new eyes and a more profound connection with God. I knew it was my mission to bring spiritual principles back into the ministry and I felt strongly guided in the endeavor. I was ready to co-create a conscious, committed community, and even though my romantic relationship had died in the entire course of my journey, I felt that I was giving birth to a deeper union with God and my creative abilities as a mystic. Little did I know that a midwife was about to appear to help with the birth of my book!

The year of my return to Unity Temple, Andrew Harvey came as a guest speaker, electrifying all of us with his wild passion. The church had come into a new era of peace and stability and many had participated in a Fall Program I had created based on Harvey's book *The Direct Path*. We had been exploring his work in Sunday Services and study groups for three months prior to the visit. I shared an overview of the work telling him of my intention to write this book. He was thrilled at the prospect and encouraged me to begin. I am grateful for his support of this book over several years. The night I began writing I felt God's blessing. One can sense this at the very depths of one's being and still continue to be awestruck when grace comes calling. I had prayed for a sign and that night I dreamed of a great tidal wave of light and knew that the Divine Mother was not only blessing my book, but calling me to write it. It is a symbol of my gratitude for her, for my teachers, for the spiritual Path, and all of its wonders.

Chapter 14

BIRTHING JOY

Meister Eckhart

*W*hen we integrate the polarities within us in the Sacred
Marriage, then we give birth to our self as a conscious creator
and that means we also give birth to joy because any time
there is a birth there is joy. The actual birth process is a metaphor for the birth of the Divine in each one of us. Whether it
is the birth of a child, an idea, a work of art, a meal, or a new
way of being, it is the birth of our self as creator. Every time
we engage in a creative act, there is the potential for joy.

Joy is an internal process grounded in spiritual truth. It is
a state of being, knowing that all is well whatever the outer

appearance. Unlike happiness, which disappears with the next drama, joy is ever-present.

I have felt joy in birthing my creative gifts, but the most indescribable joy of my life was the experience of giving birth to each of my sons, born nearly seven years apart. Christopher came to me when I was twenty eight years old, after a pregnancy filled with dreams in which he whispered his name and showed me who he would be as a child. Because of female complications prior to any knowledge that I was pregnant, along with an old fashioned naturopathic doctor, it became very difficult to determine a correct delivery date. I was expecting Chris in late November, and he surprised me on October 2, 1976. I was to have purchased supplies for a home birth at least forty five days prior to his expected arrival, sterilizing sheets and linens in advance. The morning of the 2nd, consciously believing that I was right on schedule, I bought the supplies and because fall was in the air, I turned on the heat in my house for the first time after the summer season.

While dressing to have dinner with a girlfriend that night, my water broke, and fortunately the doctor, whose office was an hour south, happened to be in the area. He brought his wife along and while the doctor meditated in the living room, his wife, a registered nurse, assisted me in the early stages. Because my husband and I were separated, my mother was my birth coach. We had only taken one class, believing we still had another month and a half to prepare, so the nurse taught us as we went, while my aunt worked frantically to sterilize supplies in the kitchen! At the stage of transition, the doctor finally came and helped my son enter the world.

It took four and a half hours for the entire delivery, and Chris arrived all powdery white, looking around with great curiosity. I was grateful that my mother was there to witness the fact that he looked up and smiled, showing his dimples from almost the first moment. To this day I think of him as intensely curious with a great sense of humor. He is nearing 30 years old as I write this and has the same good-natured disposition that he had as a child. He continues to be a great joy in my life.

Chris did not feel too joyful, however, when his younger brother Justin arrived. Actually, he did at first—he was so excited to have a new baby brother— and then about two weeks later he came to me and said, "Mom, I want to send this baby back where he came from!" Chris fell in love, though, and decided to keep his little brother Justin, and through the years they have come to deeply love and appreciate one another.

Justin's birth was very different because I was remarried and able to share the experience with his father, Clark. I was thirty five this time and because I was already a mother I was more cautious and chose to have Justin in a birthing room in the hospital rather than at home. It proved to be very fortunate, because as it became obvious that the baby was under stress, we had to even forego the simulated appearance of homebirth for emergency delivery. Justin emerged five hours later with the umbilical cord wrapped around his neck. I still remember the doctor quickly unwinding it and setting him on my stomach. I barely had time to stroke him and notice the light red fuzz on his head, before he was whisked away to my great frustration. Then I realized from across the room that he was very quiet and the doctors and nurses were hovering around him, trying to invoke the cry that would fill his lungs with air. When it finally came, I exhaled in relief and watched in slow motion as his father returned him to me.

In some ways his birth was a foreshadowing, since I have had more periods of physical separation from Justin. His father and I divorced and ended up living in separate states when Justin was seven and Chris was a young teenager. During those years both of them would spend the summers with their dad in the Midwest. But when Justin was fourteen, the visits were reversed, as he went to live with his dad in North Dakota for the school years and came to visit me in the summers. I missed him terribly since he was my other joy, along with Chris, and his kind sensitivity has always been a healing balm for me.

Both Chris and Justin actually had the opportunity to reconnect after some years of living apart. Just prior to the 2002 fall program in my church where we engaged in a community journey through The Direct Path, an interesting event occurred in my life. Justin, nineteen at the time, returned to live with his brother Chris and me, after having spent the five years with his dad in North Dakota, where he graduated from high school. He arrived and completed his first semester of college in Santa Cruz, and then moved away to attend school in another state. His brief time at home was healing for all of us since we had missed each other deeply through the years.

This condensed process in the church program, of *Falling in Love, Engagement, Sacred Marriage,* and *Birthing* ended up for me involving the deepening of my relationship with my son, and then birthing him once again back into the world on his own journey.

We are all birthers whether or not we are parents. Each of us has been gifted with amazing creative abilities. Birthing is about being a co-creator in and with God of a new integral sacred reality. We are instruments through which the Divine Artist expresses.

We each grow more brightly into birthers and accept the truth of ourselves as co-creators with God. This includes great joy and beauty and also awesome responsibility that can overwhelm us, for we tend to fear the birthing of our own creativity.

The patriarchal culture has feared the idea of birthing and has invested much in trying to control it. As a result, so many people say that they are not creative. We have associated creativity with being a painter, a sculptor, a musician, an artist in the traditional sense, but creativity is inherent in all that we do. Our life is a work of art, and we are midwives to our own joy and creative powers. Both men and women have an unlimited power of creativity and the capacity to give birth.

When we become fearful of birthing any creative idea or endeavor, we might consider the metaphor of the actual birth experience:

> The transition stage of labor is the interval during which the cervix goes from 7 centimeters to complete dilation (10 centimeters). During this time the mother usually notes a drastic change and may respond by getting very anxious, and if she is not properly supported and prepared, she may feel panic. As in the early stages of labor, she can assist only by relaxing. If she loses control, fights the contractions, she will increase her own fear, which in turn increases her discomfort. For most women, this is the most difficult stage because the interlude seems to threaten the loss of control and, momentarily at least, to be without fruit.[2]

The birth process requires a complete surrender. Once we relax and allow the natural process to occur, then we can know the resulting joy and become a truly effective co-creator.

Two specific ways to birth joy are:

1) Surrendering to the Divine creation—especially in nature.

2) Surrendering to our own creativity.

We can surrender to the Divine creation by spending time in nature whenever we need a joy break. We can walk outside, deeply inhale the air, smell the flowers, and absorb the many shades of colors in the trees, the grass, the plants, and sky. We can caress the bark of a tree and then consider that this is one place on an entire planet of beauty, and we are one small planet amidst a solar system, which is in one galaxy amidst trillions. How can we not be overwhelmed with joy?

The choice is ours: Are we going to use our creative powers to obsess about the news and worry? Or are we going to use our creative powers to focus on the wonder of creation and to be a creator ourselves?

Secondly, we can surrender to our own creativity by doing something that we love to do. Whether it is planting our garden, cooking a meal, writing a story, working on a car, building a room, or simply paying the bills, we do it with a sense of joy!

We have all of the creative power of the universe available to us right now. That power is greater than our fears which often come from our shadow side, expressing the unconscious beliefs we carry around within us. But we also have a bright shadow that is all of the good we project onto others. We admire the talent or the creativity of others as well as the capacity for joy. But we could not see it in them if it did not also exist in us. It does not mean that we can paint like Leonardo, necessarily, but the same power, the same energy is in us to be used according to our unique gifts and talents. It is never too late to activate our joy through our amazing creative powers.

Whether we are engaged in partnership or whether we are alone—we still have the potential to give birth when we open ourselves to the vast pulse of the love of God—the Spirit of the Universe—and create our lives as a work of art and a birthing of joy.

Spiritual Practice

Birthing Joy

Prayer

Call upon the Divine Mother to awaken your spiritual power of joy and fill you with bliss. Affirm: *"I am alive with the power of joy."*

Meditation

Meditate upon the idea of birth. What do you long to give birth to? Imagine your favorite form of the Divine Mother standing above you, pouring her radiant golden light into every cell of your body, filling you with joy.

Physical Activity

Choose a specific activity: plant a garden, cook a meal, or do something else that you absolutely love with an intentional spirit of joy.

Journaling

Write about what "birthing joy" would look like for you.

Chapter 15

BIRTHING THE COSMIC HEART

Back in 1957 a group of monks from a monastery had to relocate a clay Buddha from their temple to a new location. The monastery was to be relocated to make room for the development of a highway through Bangkok. When the crane began to lift the giant idol, the weight of it was so tremendous that it began to crack. What's more, rain began to fall. The head monk, who was concerned about damage to the sacred Buddha, decided to lower the statue back to the ground and cover it with a large canvas tarp to protect it from the rain.

Later that evening the head monk went to check on the Buddha. He shined his flashlight under the tarp to see if the Buddha was staying dry. As the light reached the crack, he noticed a little gleam shining back and thought it strange. As he took a closer look at this gleam of light, he wondered if there might be something underneath the clay. He went to fetch a chisel and hammer from the monastery and began to chip away at the clay. As he knocked off shards of clay, the little gleam grew brighter and bigger. Many hours of labor went by before the monk stood face to face with the extraordinary solid-gold Buddha.

Historians believe that several hundred years before the head monk's discovery, the Burmese army was about to invade Thailand (then called Siam). The Siamese monks, realizing that their country would soon be attacked, covered their precious golden Buddha with an outer covering of clay in order to keep their treasure from being looted by the Burmese. Unfortunately, it appears that the Burmese slaughtered all the Siamese monks, and the well-kept secret of the golden Buddha remained intact until that fateful day in 1957.

...We are all like the clay Buddha covered with a shell of hardness created out of fear, and yet underneath each of us is a "golden Buddha," a "golden Christ," or a "golden essence," which is our real self. Somewhere along the way... we begin to cover up our "golden essence," our natural self. Much like the monk with the hammer and chisel, our task now is to discover our true essence once again.[1]

*O*ur true essence is love. Love does make the world go 'round. It is the power of gravity calling all beings and all things to unite. Love is the harmonizing and attracting power of the universe, and our own unique Path helps us give birth to a more cosmic love.

There is a scene in Scripture where David, the great lover, enters into Jerusalem as King and he is so delighted because the Ark of the Covenant, containing the Ten Commandments, the law, is coming into the city. And David took off his clothes and danced naked in the street for sheer joy "leaping and dancing before the lord."[2]

It is this idea of awakening passion and Eros as we bring the ark—the truth—into our hearts, and open to the power of love; it makes us dance. It invokes pure Eros. Love is the dance and we can ask ourselves what kind of experiences have we had with Eros? Like David, each of us has had stops and starts, ups and downs, ins and outs, that have not looked like the image that we think of when we contemplate the romanticized ideas of love. In the book *Awakening the Heroes Within*, Carol Pearson refers to Eros as "attachment, as bonded-ness that is deeply primal and physical, as the embodiment of love, as sensual love." It is a very wide embrace. We know Eros when we experience a passionate connection to a landscape, to our work, to a cause, a religion, or a way of life. We know Eros is at work when our connection with something is so strong that the thought of losing it brings intolerable pain. It is Eros—passion, attachment, desire, even lust that makes us really alive.[3]

But in our everyday lives we mostly experience Eros as a small narrow stream of love. Then we demand that it fit certain conditions, and it certainly needs to be reciprocated in kind. Perhaps you can relate to some of my adventures that could be typified by that wonderful country western song, "Looking for Love in all the Wrong Places."

But Eros calls us to a profound experience of God's love— of God's love in us. There is a passage from a book by Frank Andrews called *The Art and Practice of Loving* that says, "It is the lover rather than the loved one who has the heartwarming experiences. The loved one is at most a stimulus. The lover is the artist who takes that stimulus and paints awe or celebration out of it." That truly is awakening the cosmic heart.

The lover is the artist who takes that movement of God inside and paints awe and celebration—or paints tragedy and doom and gloom. But we have the choice to paint awe and celebration. Lovers do not need to have their value affirmed by others. They know the value of their lives through their loving experiences. So even if love is not reciprocated, what if all of our love, no matter what, could still be full and satisfying and affirming and yes-saying to the presence of God?

We then call out the broader more cosmic dance of love that is plenty, simply because it is. Not because of any appearance in the outer world, but just because God moved in us in this way, and this is enough.

We think of Eros as involving the body and Agape as involving more of the spiritual love. For me a powerful encounter with Eros was the love at first sight experience I described in *Chapter 9*. I was struck by the arrow of the gods while looking at an inappropriate person. The liberation for me was when I said "no" and finally, at long last, released it. However, there were deep and passionate lessons given by Eros.

Ultimately it is Eros that wakes us up to feel the suffering of the earth. The denial of Eros has led to a culture in which our ultimate interconnectedness is denied. My love experience taught me that the lightning bolt—the arrow of the gods—is real. Sometimes it works out and sometimes it does not, but the wonder is the love we feel, the powerful experience of Eros, and the lessons we learn from it.

To live by love is to accept that all love is a gift and there is an invitation for a broad embrace of the dance itself. It is the denial of Eros as a vaster experience that keeps us from reaping the gifts, that keeps us from enjoying life in a much fuller, more expansive way.

The denial of Eros is very much among us; it is related to the spirit/matter split. We sometimes think that real love is abstract or pristine, or our bodies cannot be trusted. It is another manifestation of this constriction of love when in truth love invites us to something expansive and very erotic. The life of our bodies in terms of our wisdom and our love is profound. And we have split ourselves off from a source of sacred wisdom that is enormous. We need to be brave and strong in reuniting ourselves in this way, in bringing Eros back into our own lives. It has been lost in our churches for the last 2,000 years where we have been worshipping from the neck up.

I remember when I hosted the theologian Matthew Fox in my church in Tempe, Arizona. During lunch with him he said to me, "For Unity to come into its fullness it must bring the body back into worship." It was interesting because later when I attended his school in Oakland, the University of Creation Spirituality—also now called Naropa, Oakland, my Master's class had a weekend where we were taught by the youth. There were twenty year olds teaching the class and they took us on a tour of their ritual center down the block from the school. They had just purchased The Old Newberry Bldg—which houses the Sweets Ballroom, the first place Frank Sinatra ever sang in Oakland. It is operational now, but back then we had to enter with a flashlight in the dark up a flight of stairs, and when we rounded a corner, there was a giant ballroom—66,000 square feet in this building. This entire space was to be devoted to youth and bringing the body back into worship. And that means a lot of dance, and we danced, even to a song called *When David Danced*. Bringing the body back into worship is so essential for us.

Dawn Cartwright, one of my fellow students in Oakland, wrote a poem:

I want to dance, to dance, to dance

Right outside, outside, outside

Outside my mask

I want to voice, to voice, to voice

To voice my voice

God looks down, winks and says,

Baby it's your choice.

I want to open like a flood

To spin and scream

And play in my own mud

I want to dance, to dance, to dance

Right outside, outside, outside,

Outside my mask

I want to run naked down the street

Just to see what like-minded spirits I might meet

I want to voice, to voice, to voice,

To voice my voice.

God looks down, winks and says,

Baby it's your choice.[4]

It is always a choice to expand our consciousness, to open our hearts, to breathe deeply and feel in our bodies the experience of *yes*, the experience of the dance.

Kids, from the beginning, seem to be in touch with the dance of love, the golden essence, and self love.

> A little boy was overheard talking to himself as he strode through his backyard, baseball cap in place and toting ball and bat. "I'm the greatest baseball player in the world," he said proudly. Then he tossed the ball in the air, swung and missed. Undaunted, he picked up the ball, threw it into the air and said to himself, "I'm the greatest player ever!" He swung at the ball again, and again he missed. He paused a moment to examine bat and ball carefully. Then once again he threw the ball into the air and said, "I'm the greatest baseball player who ever lived." He swung the bat hard and again missed the ball.
>
> Wow!" he exclaimed. "What a pitcher! [5]

Self love can occur from a change in perspective—a willingness to look at the positive in ourselves as we can often do with another. This leads us to Agape. Eros evolves into Agape when it becomes spiritual, when it is taken to a higher level.

> Love is the underlying movement and pattern behind the universe. Atoms calling each other in search of union so that they begin to constellate and form molecules. Molecules in resonance yearning for the beloved of the next stage so they can form more complex systems. These systems yearning to form bodies, bodies attuning until they find their partner have produced more bodies with

more complexities.

> We yearn for the gods and the gods yearn for us, so that as we are becoming enspirited godded beings the gods are becoming human. Earth and nature long for spirit and spirit longs for nature and out of this longing emerges a deeply physicalized spirituality and a deeply spiritual embodiment. This embodiment is the love that moves the sun and other stars.

> So God is the Divine Lover calling the world into becoming and the search for the beloved is the lure of human becoming and this is the essence of agape."[6]

We expand love beyond the notion that it is an object, like another person, or that it is an event, like once in a lifetime. We recognize it as the very ground of our being, the very essence of what calls our cells into the dance. It is a sense of belonging in the great scheme of things and that manifests at times as belonging in relationship to another person. But it is first of all, belonging.

Maya Angelou said, "Not only do I belong, I am necessary." That is the essence of love in its deepest sense, a connectedness to the whole in such a way that it values each individual's being and all of creation—in this dance.

In his book *The Way of Passion—A Celebration of Rumi,* Andrew Harvey said:

> When your heart has been purified, the Sufis say, the eye of the heart opens and that eye sees the Beloved in

every person, in every blade of grass, the shining of the shining in every event and every action.

The Christians would say that when you have been Christed, you will experience reality as Christ and you will love reality with Christ's heart, you will taste reality with Christ's mouth, and suffer with Christ's love, and long with Christ's longing. But Christ is not out there, Christ is here waiting to be unfolded and waiting to be lived completely in you!"[7]

Let us behold the Christ within and without, giving birth to a greater cosmic heart as the Lovers that we are.

Birthing the Cosmic Heart

Prayer

Invoke the Presence of the Divine Mother, calling upon her power of love and grace to manifest in your life and in the world. Affirm: "*I am an expression of Divine love and grace.*"

Meditation

Sit quietly and relax in the Silence. Ask the Mother to reveal how and where you can best help the planet with your love. Listen for her answer.

Physical Activity

Treat yourself to a massage, a sauna, a swim, or some other experience where you feel nurtured. Let it be part of an entire afternoon of self love.

Journaling

Take time to write what you have learned about love. What does the expression "Cosmic Heart" mean to you?

Chapter 16

BIRTHING A NEW WORLD

*T*he path we have walked has led us to the present moment. We are at the center of creation and it is now imperative that we use our wisdom and creative abilities to make a profound difference. Each one of us must ask ourselves the questions:

"How can I give birth to myself as a conscious co-creator?"

"How can I give birth to an enlightened and compassionate humanity?"

"How can I save our species and transform the world?"

We have a map to guide us, a powerful framework that helps us to discover and understand our past and our future. When we see our current personal and collective dilemma in the context of Falling in Love, Engagement, Sacred Marriage, and Birthing, our path becomes clear.

Transformative change includes:

1) Cultivating a state of being, a deeper sense of awe and wonder and connection with God *(Falling in Love)*

2) Facing the darkness, the pain, and the testing with deep intention *(Engagement)*

3) Affirming the creation of a new mythology, a new paradigm *(Sacred Marriage)*

4) Taking compassionate action to help the world *(Birthing)*

CULTIVATING A STATE OF BEING *(Falling In Love)*

The framework of the Direct Path actually becomes our remedy for the dilemma of healing the world. We must begin by falling in love with creation and knowing that we have been blessed from the beginning for billions of years. We are born in blessing and all of life is a gift and God is the Source.

Matthew Fox said:

> God has laid an egg. A beautiful, delicate, organic, developing and life-filled egg. It is our home. We call it the global village. ....Unlike any generation to precede us, we have taken a look at its beauty—in our times there has occurred an unprecedented breakthrough in our awareness and appreciation of the world egg. That breakthrough is in the form of photographs taken by astronauts miles from our global village. What we see

through this picture no human beings in the entire history of the world have ever seen before. It is the oneness, the unity, the harmony and balance of our global village. It is truly a new mandala, this picture we all share of the globe on which we live. The word "mandala" comes from the Sanskrit word for circle or center. A mandala is a sacred circle which is meant to heal us, to make us whole and as holy as we truly are. ...There are many mandalas in our lives—atoms, the eye, the body, flowers, the DNA, when viewed from the top. To meditate on a mandala is to get in touch quite literally with our roots as living organisms since every cell is a mandala.....The world egg, (our) global village (is) fighting to breathe as a single organism, a unity struggling, like a newly hatched egg, to survive. ...And, like any true mandala, this global village is not merely 'out there' but is in us at the same time that we are in it."...The healing of the New Mandala—the Global Village known as the World Egg—takes place together with the healing of the human egg—the soul....or it does not take place at all."[1]

It reminds me of a story about a teacher who had to deal with a recalcitrant student. She tears up this map of the world and gives it to a small boy to keep him busy and tells him to put it together again. She thinks it will take him a long time but he comes back in a few minutes with it all together. She is amazed and asks him how he could have done this. He responds, "Well it was easy because there was a torn apart person on the back and I just put the person together and then the whole world came together."[2]

This is a wonderful image for us because it is true that as we find the Divinity within, we help birth the healing of the planet. We must cultivate a state of being, knowing that we are one with God and the preciousness of life in the cosmic community called the world egg.

Cultivating that consciousness of oneness helps love to blossom wherever we go. For example, some very interesting information has come to light through the work of a pioneering nurse named Carol Montgomery who is associated with the University of Colorado. She wanted to find out how "deeply caring" nurses remained healthy while maintaining close relationships with the patients they served. Carol knew that caregivers had been taught and lived by the premise that they were supposed to care deeply for their clients while not getting too involved because of the very real potential of burnout.

In interviewing those nurses who had a reputation for being seasoned experts at caring, she discovered, that they "did nothing" in particular that was caring. It was their genuine sense of presence, of being, rather than doing, which established a deep bond between nurse and patient. By letting this be the form of interaction, the nurses found themselves uplifted and nurtured with an expanded ability to tap into energy, love and wisdom. They did not find themselves depleted or burned out by their deep, caring close relationship.

As we foster this loving presence or being, through spiritual practice, prayer, and meditation…falling in love with God…then we change our own personal stories and we also help the greater community.

FACING THE DARKNESS WITH DEEP INTENTION
(Engagement)

We truly cannot help ourselves or others until we are willing to enter the darkness, the pain, and the suffering. With the deepest intention to serve, we must consciously feel our feelings about the losses taking place in our world. We can no longer afford to ignore the facts.

This is a time of complete disintegration. Everything is breaking down politically, socially, economically, and religiously. It is important that we recognize that we cannot depend upon old structures to sustain us.

Our environment is being destroyed at an alarming rate, from ozone depletion and the permanent destruction of ecosystems, to unchecked global warming that threatens the planet with melting polar ice caps, the rise of sea levels, floods, drought, and disease. The destruction of the world's rain forests can destabilize planetary climactic conditions; while the loss of plant and animal life deprives suffering humanity of essential food, medicine, and shelter. Government response is completely inadequate and now we must become our own saviors as we stand on the edge of the precipice.

Our species is at a critical brink as the world polarizes

between the two movements of capitalism and ecology, and between the old religious model of obedience, and the power of creativity. That which we love is threatened, and we must shift from complacency to action, according to our own guidance and Truth. Denial is still rampant, however, even among those on a conscious spiritual path. The tendency to focus on the positive is certainly beneficial in daily living, but it has become our nemesis, as we avoid the dark truth that the collective shadow brings. This is why the Direct Path to God is so important, because when we have traversed the stages, we are awakened to those pitfalls and we see with shocking clarity what must transpire for the greater good. This journey has never been more important for each one of us. We must stop pretending that all is well, look around, and take full grasp of the consequences we face.

Now is the time! That which we love IS threatened.

Capitalism, like a virus, infects us with a prevailing belief that life is a commodity and the "bottom line" is of foremost importance. The corrupt corporations of today are like the cults of yesterday. They imprison minds and souls and are equally dangerous. Employees who leave them have the same exact symptoms of those who escape a cult, for they must deprogram themselves from the brainwashing that occurs. They have been taught a language and a set of beliefs and over time, they have become exhausted by the common myth that speed and long hours create success. The prize in a typical spiritual cult is supposed to be God, and in the corporation, that God is money, often at the expense of ethics and one's soul, as well as the world environment. It is not only the employees who suffer, but everyone in the culture, for the corporation has become the dominant institutional structure, and is accountable to no one. To make matters worse, corporations now control the media and determine the news, which means that our freedom is seriously jeopardized.

Ecology, on the other hand, is concerned with a consciousness of all life. The preserving of creation supersedes the greed of ego, and emphasizes the power of one person as well as an entire community to make a difference. Eco-design is the wave of the future, and ecology groups will become an even greater force in our world than any current political parties. With that power they will be challenged to remain true to their mission, and it will take tremendous strength.

Not only do the movements of capitalism and ecology appear to be polarized, but also religious obedience and creativity. A model of religious obedience causes the need to obey rather than question. We are then guided by blind faith, rather than by an understanding faith based on applied principle. We are told to believe literal interpretations of Scripture, and to forego the deeper truths to be found in metaphor. When adults behave as unquestioning obedient children, they are gullible and are easily deceived by corrupt politicians, corporate executive officers, spiritual leaders, or anyone who is able to manipulate the message within the context of a person's belief system. People have even obeyed orders to kill and torture others "in the name of" whatever God or spiritual being they worship. It is amazing how some people can apply their intellect in most aspects of their lives, and yet abandon all rational thought about their religion.

The model of religious obedience also results in fundamentalism. This is not describing a specific religion, but rather a fanaticism that crosses all denominational lines. Fundamentalists believe that their path is the "only way," and that others must be converted, sometimes even forcefully. There is little tolerance for differences and a self righteousness that excludes and separates people.

Creativity, however, involves a willingness to go beyond rational constructs into the realm of intuition and possibility. The head and the heart are joined in a new birth where old models are discarded as new paradigms and world views are born. This is the realm of imagination where we see there is no separation in truth and we envision the future we would like to create. Even as we directly face the challenges, so too can we begin to imagine new ways of being in the world and to know that our thoughts are prayers. Then we must "put wings on our prayers" by acting on the guidance we receive.

Even the archetypal model of the Path to God, as shown to us by Jesus and the other mystics of the ages, can dissolve in the light of new realization and effort. Jesus reminded us, "The things which I do, you can do also, and even greater things."[3] There will be a time when we do not have to pursue the same path as those enlightened beings that went before us. I believe they made a willing sacrifice, pointing to an even more sublime state of being for us, one that is free from suffering…where the path, having served its purpose falls away and life becomes the experience of Heaven on Earth.

Until that time, we must be willing to face the truth. But even with our awareness we have a dilemma that is described in the following myth:

> Beautiful Cassandra was the youngest daughter of the last King of Troy. The god Apollo fell in love with her, but she refused him. To win her affections, he made a proposal: If she agreed to love him, he would give her the gift of prophecy.
>
> Cassandra accepted the bargain, and she was graced with the ability to see the future. But she could not bring herself to love Apollo after all. Apollo was filled with outrage. Though Cassandra's gift could not be taken back, the god revenged himself in the most cruel way imaginable. He begged her for a single kiss, and she consented. When their lips touched, Apollo breathed into Cassandra's mouth in such a way that no one would ever believe her prophesies.
>
> Cassandra was thus doomed to a life of despair. She could see the dangers threatening others, but she could not prevent them. Cassandra warned the Trojans that the Greeks were about to attack, and she cried out to warn them that soldiers were hidden inside the Trojan Horse. But her warnings went unheeded. Troy collapsed under the Greek onslaught.

Captured, she was taken back to Greece. Her reputation as a seer came with her, as did Apollo's curse. "What do you know about the future?" they taunted her. She foretold a palace murder, and her own death, and that both would happen before sundown. The Greeks scoffed.

Before the end of the day, everything came to pass exactly as Cassandra had foreseen…

In the long run, perhaps it was all for the good. Why? Because we can learn from the story, even if it did not actually occur. Cassandra's dilemma is a myth…that most likely did not happen, but it conveys a truth that we can relate to in our world today.

Consultant and author Alan Atkisson said,

To understand that humanity is on a collision course with the laws of Nature is to be stuck in Cassandra's Dilemma. One may be able to see the most likely outcome of current trends. One can warn people about what is happening, and underscore the need for a change in course.

Some people can understand, and a few may even believe it and try to take action—but the vast majority cannot, or will not, respond.

The Cassandra's in this case, may be laughed at if it ends up being false, called incompetent prophets, or if it all comes to pass, they could even be blamed. Certainly the worst and most painful outcome for any Cassandra is to be proven right.[4]

This is an interesting myth that lives in our world today. The more recent prophecies began with a few lone voices... Rachel Carson in her book *Silent Spring*, for example, and that was before there was an ecological movement. Now today, we are hearing it everywhere we turn...from the scientific communities and even the media.

Woody Allen said, "More than any other time in history, mankind faces the crossroads... one path leads to despair and utter hopelessness, the other to total extinction. I pray we have the wisdom to choose wisely."[5]

AFFIRMING THE CREATION OF A NEW MYTHOLOGY (*Sacred Marriage*)

It is time to access our wisdom and create a new story that unites the polarities. Mythologists like Joseph Campbell have said that we are in profound need of a new mythology. Our world is now changing so fast that many of our institutions, as well as our old stories and beliefs, are becoming irrelevant and can no longer serve to guide us. We find ourselves in new territory in a changing world, which is becoming smaller all the time.

We now know what the mystics have told us from the beginning...that we are all one, interconnected in a great web of life. It probably is, in fact, true that the flutter of a butterfly's wing can be felt in a distant galaxy. At least we are beginning to believe that. So our new mythology, or way of being in the world, must take into account the fact that we are all part of a global community.

What can we do to create new stories or myths?

This is an idea I have wrestled with for a long time in the business of church. For awhile I was a Peace Worker with the Association of Unity Churches, and going into different con-flicted churches taught me that there is generally a repeating story....the community is caught in a theme that continues to replay. One person can leave, and another will arrive and it is as though he or she auditioned for the part and was hired to play it. Sometimes if a church community has issues of power and co-dependence, then it will become an addictive organi-zation. I attempted to assist one church with a twelve person board, where a Board Member was a practicing alcoholic, and one half of the board knew, and the other half did not. Those who knew were trying to protect everyone else. These types of themes tend to repeat in one form or another.

I learned that the size of the community is not important, but the power is in the stories that continue to be told. That applies in our own individual lives, in our communities and in our world. We can see history repeat itself personally and collectively.

To change a myth in a community, for example, there must be strong leadership, where those at the helm are willing to hold a positive vision and stay on course...amidst "the slings and arrows of outrageous fortune," so to speak.

In our personal lives we cannot burst into our family reunions or our community circles and say, "Now listen up...

we are going to start telling ourselves positive new stories!" It is not that easy to simply forget about the abuse in the family, or the terror in the world community, and move on. In creating a new story, we do not ignore the problem...or pretend it does not exist...we face it, take the necessary action, and then we invoke and affirm a more positive story.

Myrtle Fillmore, co-founder of Unity, is my great role model of this idea. She was dying of tuberculosis, but she heard the words, "You are a child of God, and therefore you do not inherit sickness." And she held on to that new story. It was a greater more positive truth than the old one that said she had inherited her disease.

Did she simply pretend the old story had no effect? No, she did not deny it...she went into the diseased parts...faced them, and then sent them love...sent strength and energy and power to the organs of her body each day. If she had been in denial, she would have pretended the problem did not exist.

Likewise, entering into a troubled community one would not deny the effects of the past history. That must be faced and dealt with, even while the new story, the new vision is being spoken and acted out. And the new story must allow people to understand that even the past history has been a part of the healing journey.

Each one of us has the power to transform the old stories and systems by confronting the challenge, whatever it is...and affirming a new story, a new mythology. Imagine in detail the vision and fulfillment of your heart's desire in both the personal and collective circumstance.

TAKING COMPASSIONATE ACTION TO HELP
(Birthing)

After lecturing her 6 year old on the golden rule, a mother concluded, "Always remember that we are in this world to help others." The little girl mulled this over for a minute and then asked, "What are the others here for?"[6]

Myrtle Fillmore healed herself, but she did not stop there. She asked God what she could do...and she began to pray with people...and they were healed also. It was her gift, and she went on to help create what today is the Unity Movement. It is amazing how one person expressing a spiritual presence or state of being, can affect the whole...and especially as we begin to serve and help others beyond our selves.

Rosemary Fillmore-Rhea, the granddaughter of Myrtle and Charles Fillmore, in her beautiful memoir, *That's Just How My Spirit Travels*, carries on the tradition. She said, "The old paradigms will not work in a changing universe. The challenges facing our world today cannot be solved in the same consciousness in which they have been created. Life is demanding that we think in higher categories. To survive as a human species, we must learn finally and forevermore that violence begets violence, and the eye-for-an-eye morality, as Gandhi so aptly said, ends in a world of darkness. The urgency of this time calls for a revolution of consciousness. Revolutionary times demand revolutionary thinking."

She goes on to say, "Charles Fillmore was a revolutionary thinker. We forget that sometimes because so many of the things he taught—like the role the mind plays in causing illness and the power of positive thinking, to mention two—are now widely accepted. But in the beginning, he was considered shocking and was often condemned by established religions."

He wrote: "All reforms must begin with their cause. Their cause is mind, and mind does all its work in the realm of silence, which, in reality, is the only realm where sound and power go hand in hand…all philosophers and sages have recognized this silent cause, this perpetual outflow from center to circumference."[7]

We all have a deep longing to give—to give to the earth, to one another, and to the greater community. We long to work and to love in order to care for this earth. We long to unite the polarities within and without. That is true for every human being even if we still have yet to discover it.

Robert Johnson suggests a powerful healing image for us as we unite our polarities and create a new mythology in the world. It is called a mandorla. It is different than a mandala. It is that almond-shaped segment that is made when two circles partly overlap. It is not by chance that mandorla is also the Italian word for almond. This symbol signifies nothing less than the overlap of opposites, generally described as the overlap of heaven and earth. The mandorla instructs us how to give birth to reconciliation…within ourselves and the world.

When one is tired or discouraged or so battered by life that one can no longer live in the tension of the opposites, the mandorla begins the healing of the split. It is the new birth that emerges....the place of poetry that unites the beauty and the terror of existence. It reminds us that we can move beyond dualism and contradiction to paradox and unity.

All good stories are mandorlas. They speak of this and that and gradually, through the miracle of story, demonstrate that the opposites overlap and are finally the same. We like to think that a story is based on the triumph of good over evil; but the deeper truth is that good and evil are superseded and the two become one. Since our capacity for synthesis is limited, many stories can only hint at this unity. But any unity, even a hint, is healing.[8]

I am reminded of a story that is a perfect mandorla:

When the great creator Leonardo Da Vinci painted the Last Supper, the time engaged for its completion was seven years. The figures representing the twelve Apostles and Jesus himself were painted from living persons. The life-model for the painting of the figure of Jesus was chosen first.

When it was decided that Da Vinci would paint this great picture, hundreds and hundreds of young men were carefully viewed in an endeavor to find a face and personality exhibiting sweetness, innocence and beauty.

Finally after weeks of laborious search, a young man nineteen years of age was selected as a model for the portrayal of Christ. For six months Da Vinci worked on the production of this leading character of his famous painting.

During the next six years Da Vinci continued his labors on this sublime work of art. One by one fitting persons were chosen to represent each of the eleven Apostles; space being left for the painting of the figure representing Judas Iscariot, as the final task of this masterpiece. This was the Apostle, you remember, who betrayed Jesus for 30 pieces of silver.

For weeks Da Vinci searched for a man with a hard, callous face, with a countenance marked by scars of avarice, deceit, hopocrisy and crime; a face that would delineate a character who would betray his best friend.

Word finally came to Da Vinci that a man whose appearance met his requirements had been found in a dungeon in Rome, sentenced to die for a life of crime and murder.

Da Vinci made the trip to Rome at once, and this man was brought out from the dungeon and led out into the light of the sun. There Da Vinci saw before him a dark, swarthy man, his long shaggy and unkempt hair, sprawled over his face which betrayed a character of complete ruin. At last the famous painter had found the person he wanted to represent Judas.

By special permission from the king, this prisoner was carried to Milan where the picture was being painted; and for months he sat before Da Vinci at appointed hours each day as the gifted artist continued his painting. As he finally finished his last stroke, he turned to the guards and said, "I have finished. You may take the prisoner away."

As the guards were leading their prisoner away, he suddenly broke loose from their control and rushed up to Da Vinci, crying as he did so, "O, Da Vinci, look at me! Do you not know who I am?"

Da Vinci, with the trained eyes of a great character student, carefully scrutinized the man upon whose face he had constantly gazed for six months and replied, "No, I have never seen you in my life until you were brought out of the dungeon in Rome."

Then lifting his eyes up, the prisoner said, "Oh, God, have I fallen so low?" Then turning his face to the painter he cried, "Leonardo Da Vinci! Look at me again, for I am the same man you painted just seven years ago as the figure of Christ.[9]

Will we create or will we destroy? Whenever we have a clash of opposites in our being or in the world, and neither will give way to the other, we can be certain that God is present. Paradox is the place beyond the polarities...where we can hold both and birth that which is transcendent. One can view this story and all of human life as a mandorla...and as the ground upon which the opposites find their reconciliation. In this way every human being is a redeemer, and the Christ within, that perfect pattern of wholeness in each of us...is the prototype for this creative task.

We are at the center of the universe with all of the creative power there is available to us right now. That power is greater than any obstacles, any fears, or critical voices. It is essential for us to know that each one of us makes a difference in birthing a new world. We could make *THE* difference in creating the critical mass of Christ Consciousness, which has been called the second coming—the awakening of all humankind to our Divine potential. It therefore becomes urgent that each one of us continues our path of awakening, balancing spiritual practice with action, and galvanizing our will in order to transform and birth a new world.

> What is the test that you have indeed undergone this holy birth? Listen carefully. If this birth has truly taken place within you then no creature can any longer hinder you. Rather, every single creature points you toward God and toward this birth. You receive a rich potential for sensitivity, a magnificent vulnerability in whatever you see or hear no matter what it is you can absorb therein nothing but this birth. In fact, everything becomes for you nothing but God. For in the midst of all things you keep your eye only on God to grasp God in all things. This is the sign of your new birth.[10]

God bless you on your path!

Birthing a New World

Prayer

Pray to Mother Father God to birth a glorious new world, free from terror and greed, and radiant with an awakened humanity. Affirm: "*I now express my creative gifts and give birth to a new world.*"

Meditation

Relax in a meditative state and ask God to reveal to you what your specific work is as a mystical activist—an active change agent in the world.

Physical Activity

Take action based on your guidance and set a specific intention to fulfill your calling as an instrument of God's Will and Divine Grace in the world.

Journaling

Imagine that you are the one who will make the difference in creating critical mass in the awakening of human consciousness. Write what you intend to do about it. Now what are you waiting for?

NOTES

(Please refer to Bibliography for complete citations)

INTRODUCTION

1. Kent Nerburn, quoting Black Elk, as quoted in Angeles Arrien, PhD, *The Four-Fold Way*, 7.

2. Edward Eagle Man McGaa, *Mother Earth Spirituality*, 33.

3. Matthew Fox. *Original Blessing*, 260.

CHAPTER 2

1. Taylor-Perry, Rosemarie, *The God Who Comes*, 100.

2. From Rumi, Ode 442 "One Whisper of the Beloved."

3. Rumi, as translated by Coleman Barks et al., *The Essential Rumi*, 193.

4. I have been using this for years and do not know its source. I believe it is from kids' quotes somewhere on the Internet.

5. Jack Kornfield, *After the Ecstasy, the Laundry*, 26.

6. *Ibid.*, 27.

7. *Ibid.*, 30.

8. Frederic Brussat et al., *Spiritual Literacy*, 430-31.

CHAPTER 3

1. Gregg Levoy, *Callings*, 65.

2. Lorna Catford and Michael Ray, *The Path of the Everyday Hero*, 17.

3. Robert Johnson, *We*, xi.

4. *Ibid.*, xii – xiii.

5. *What exactly is Marriage?*
    From: www.hifunny.com/jokes/its-what-kids-think-23.php
    posted by hifunny on 10 April 2006.

6. Gregg Levoy, *Callings*, 69.

7. Charles Fillmore, *The Twelve Powers of Man*, 132.

8. Teilhard de Chardin, as quoted in Jeanne Larson and Madge Micheels-Cyrus, *Seeds of Peace*, 270.

9. Leo Buscaglia, *Born for Love*, 137.

10. From personal notes on a talk by Andrew Harvey.

11. Rumi, Mathnawi VI. 4302-4304 as found on the internet www.khamush.com/love_poems.html referenced to *Teachings of Rumi (The Masnawi): The Spiritual Couplets of Jalaluddin Rumi*, abridged and translated by E.M. Winfield, (Ohio, Oxford Press 1994).

CHAPTER 4

1. Deepak Chopra, *How to Know God*, 5.

2. Matthew Fox, *Meditations with Meister Eckhart*, 60.

3. Anthony DeMello, *Song of the Bird*, 12-13.

4. *Ibid.*, 166.

Chapter 5

1. Daniel C. Matt, *The Essential Kabbalah*, 2-7.

2. *Ibid.*, 10.

Chapter 6

1. This is a quote from the film *The Fellowship of the Ring*, based on J.R.R. Tolkien's *Lord of the Rings* trilogy.

2. Quote from the film *The Fellowship of the Ring*.

3. Gary Zukav, *Soul Stories*, 249, 252.

4. Matthew 4:3-11.

5. Quote attributed to Mark Twain. Source unknown.

6. John 19: 10-11.

7. Job 30: 16, 17, 19.

8. Evelyn Underhill, *Mysticism*, 383.

9. John 14:12.

10. Charles Fillmore, *The Twelve Powers of Man*, 15.

11. Scott Peck, *The Road Less Traveled*, 278.

12. Andrew Harvey, *The Sun at Midnight*, 221-222.

13. Elisabeth Haich, *Initiation*, 132, 133.

14. John Sanford, *Dreams: God's Forgotten Language*.

15. The great mythologist Joseph Campbell always said that all of life is a story.

16. Carl G. Jung, et al., *Memories, Dreams, Reflections*, 158-159.

17. Charles Fillmore, *Christian Healing*, 102,103.

18. James Dillet Freeman, *The Story of Unity*, 40-41.

19. Personal notes from a talk by Jeremy Taylor.

20. Matthew Fox, *The Coming of the Cosmic Christ*, 137.

21. Eckhart Tolle, *The Power of Now*, 11.

CHAPTER SEVEN

1. Hebrews 11:1.

2. James Dillet Freeman, *The Story of Unity*, 6-7.

3. The story of Myrtle Fillmore's miraculous healing as told in James Dillet Freeman, *The Story of Unity*.

4. Modern-day parable appearing in many versions; source unknown.

5. John 5:2.

6. Charles Fillmore, *Metaphysical Bible Dictionary*, 117.

7. Charles Fillmore's healing journey as told in James Dillet Freeman, *The Story of Unity*.

8. John Dear, *Mohandas Gandhi*, 73, 74.

9. James Dillet Freeman, *The Story of Unity*, 117-18.

10. Emilie Cady, *Lessons in Truth*, 64-69.

CHAPTER EIGHT

1. Genesis 1:3-4.

2. Dorothy Walter, *Unmasking the Rose*, 1.

3. The story of the magician Saruman the Wise, his turning away from the light and his ultimate demise is chronicled in the first two books of J.R.R. Tolkien's *Lord of the Rings* trilogy, *The Fellowship of the Ring* and *The Two Towers* (Mariner Books 1999).

4. Gary Zukav, *Seat of the Soul*, 95-96.

5. Adapted from Shah, Indries, *The Exploits of the Incomparable Mulla Nasruddin*, 9.

6. Matthew Fox, *Original Blessing*, 134-135.

7. I have been using this story for many years and I have not been able to locate its source.

CHAPTER NINE

1. This is a summary of the essence of the book by Robert Johnson, *We;* see Chapter 12, 105-115.

CHAPTER TEN

1. These stories were collected from various emails circulating on the internet. Some of them can be found at:
   Solid Advice on Marriage from Kids,
   http:// wilk4.com/humor/humorm48.htm

2. Leslie Temple-Thurston, *The Marriage of Spirit*, 18.

3. Matthew 22: 1-14.

4. Another amusing story that circulated by email on the internet.

5. Leslie Temple-Thurston, *The Marriage of Spirit*, 17.

6. *Ibid.*, 18

CHAPTER ELEVEN

1. Frederic Brussat et al., *Spiritual Literacy*, 471, 474.

2. *Ibid.*, 474.

3. Ram Dass and Mirabai Bush, *Compassion in Action: Setting Out on the Path of Service*, as quoted in Frederic Brussat et al. *Spiritual Literacy*, 493-94.

4. *Ibid.*, p. 494.

5. Jack Canfield, *A 2nd Helping of Chicken Soup for the Soul*, 307-308.

6. Bolles, Richard N., *How to Find Your Mission in Life*, 12-14.

7. Abridged from "The Rabbi's Gift" from *The Different Drum: Making Community and Making Peace* by M. Scott Peck (NY: Simon & Schuster Inc., 1987), 13-15.

CHAPTER TWELVE

1. E.B. White as quoted in Jack Kornfield, *After the Ecstasy, the Laundry*, 259.

2. Jack Kornfield, *After the Ecstasy, the Laundry*, 259.

3. David Whyte "The Heart Aroused," as recounted in Frederic Brussat et al., *Spiritual Literacy*, 342-343.

4. Andrew Harvey, *The Direct Path*, 60.

5. *Ibid.*, 59.

6. Matthew Fox, *Original Blessing*, 112-113.

7. An excerpt from the poem "When We Praise God", in Freeman, James Dillet, *Prayer: The Master Key*, 136.

8. Notes received in a lecture by Brian Swimme, author of *The Universe Story*.

Chapter Thirteen

1. Matthew Fox, *Meditations with Meister Eckhart*, 24.

Chapter Fourteen

1. Meister Eckhart as quoted in Matthew Fox, *Original Blessing*, 220.

2. *Ibid.*, 159.

Chapter Fifteen

1. Jack Canfield and Mark Victor Hansen, *Chicken Soup for the Soul*, 69.

2. 2 Samuel 6: 14.

3. Carol Pearson, *Awakening the Heroes Within*, 149.

4. Dawn Cartwright was a fellow student at the University of Creation Spirituality in Oakland, California. She also attended Unity Temple of Santa Cruz, where I was serving at the time. She attended a class I taught and wrote this poem. I

am grateful for the opportunity to share it in this book.

5. Jack Canfield and Mark Victor Hansen, *Chicken Soup for the Soul*, 74.

6. Teilhard de Chardin as quoted in Jean Houston, *The Search for the Beloved*, 137.

7. Andrew Harvey, *The Way of Passion*, 54.

CHAPTER SIXTEEN

1. Matthew Fox, *A Spirituality Named Compassion*, 267.

2. Quoting Soozi Holbeche in Frederic Brussat et al., *Spiritual Literacy*, 354-355.

3. John 14: 12-14

4. Alan Atkisson, *Believing Cassandra*, 22-23.

5. Jeanne Larson, *Seeds of Peace*, 76.

6. One of many quotes of children's views of life circulating in email. Source unknown.

7. Rosemary Fillmore-Rhea, *That's Just How My Spirit Travels*, 204-205.

8. Robert Johnson, *Owning Your Own Shadow*, 97-118.

9. This story appears in my family Bible (1951 King James) on an insert between pages 626 and 627, on the back of a picture of DaVinci's famous painting of The Last Supper.

10. Matthew Fox, *Meditations with Meister Eckhart*, 83.

BIBLIOGRAPHY

Andrews, Frank. (1991). *The Art and Practice of Loving*. New York: Tarcher/Putnam.

Arrien, Angeles. (1993) *The Four-Fold Way: Walking the Paths of the Warrior, Teacher, Healer & Visionary*. HarperSanFrancisco.

Atkisson, Alan. (1999) *Believing Cassandra: An Optimist Looks at a Pessimist's World*. White River Junction, Vermont: Chelsea Green Publishing.

Bolles, Richard N. (2001). *How to Find Your Mission in Life*. Berkeley/Toronto: Ten Speed Press.

Brussat, Frederic, Mary Ann Brussat, and Thomas Moore. (1996) *Spiritual Literacy: Reading the Sacred in Everyday Life*. New York: Touchstone.

Buscaglia, Leo. (1992). *Born for Love: Reflections on Loving*. New York: Ballantine Books.

Cady, H. Emilie. (1961) *Lessons in Truth: A Course of Twelve Lessons in Practical Christianity*. Unity Village, Missouri.

Campbell, Joseph. (1991). *The Power of Myth*. New York: Anchor Books.

Campbell, Joseph. (2008). (3rd Edition) *The Hero with a Thousand Faces.* New York: New World Library.

Canfield, Jack, and Mark Victor Hansen. (1993) *Chicken Soup for the Soul: 101 Stories to Open the Heart and Rekindle the Spirit.* Deerfield Beach, FL: Health Communications Inc.

Canfield, Jack, and Mark Victor Hansen. (1995) *A 2nd Helping of Chicken Soup for the Soul: 101 More Stories to Open the Heart and Rekindle the Spirit.* Deerfield Beach, FL: Health Communications Inc.

Catford, Lorna, and Michael Ray. (1991). *The Path of the Everyday Hero: Drawing on the Power of Myth to Meet Life's Most Important Challenges.* Forestville, CA: Creative Quest Publishing.

Chopra, Deepak. (2000). *How to Know God: The Soul's Journey into the Mystery of Mysteries.* New York: Three Rivers Press.

Dear, John, ed. (2002). *Mohandas Gandhi: Essential Writings.* Maryknoll, New York: Orbis Books.

DeMello, Anthony. (1984). *Song of the Bird.* New York: Doubleday.

The Essential Rumi. (1995). Translated by Coleman Barks with John Moyne, A.J. Arberry and Reynold Nicholson. New York: Castle Books (HarperCollins).

Fillmore, Charles. (1949) *Christian Healing.* Kansas City, MO: Unity School of Christianity.

Fillmore, Charles. (2000) *Metaphysical Bible Dictionary.* Unity Village, MO: Unity Books.

Fillmore, Charles. (1930) *The Twelve Powers of Man.* Unity Village, MO: Unity Books.

Fillmore-Rhea, Rosemary. (2003) *That's Just How My Spirit Travels.* Unity Village, MO: Unity Books.

Fox, Matthew. (1988) *The Coming of the Cosmic Christ.* San Francisco: Harper & Row.

Fox, Matthew. (1983) *Meditations with Meister Eckhart: The Path is Beautiful and Pleasant and Joyful and Familiar.* Santa Fe, NM: Bear & Company.

Fox, Matthew. (1999). *A Spirituality Named Compassion: Uniting Mystical Awareness with Social Justice.* Rochester, Vermont: Inner Traditions.

Fox, Matthew. (2000) *Original Blessing: A Primer in Creation Spirituality Presented in Four Paths, Twenty-Six Themes, and Two Questions.* New York: Tarcher/Putnam.

Freeman, James Dillet. (1968). *Prayer: The Master Key.* Unity Village MO: Unity Books.

Freeman, James Dillet. (1985/1991). *The Story of Unity.* Unity Village MO: Unity Books.

Haich, Elisabeth. (2000). *Initiation.* Santa Fe, NM: Aurora Press.

Harvey, Andrew. (2000). *The Way of Passion: A Celebration of Rumi.* New York: Tarcher/Putnam.

Harvey, Andrew. (2001). *The Direct Path: Creating a Personal Journey to the Divine Using the World's Spiritual Traditions.* New York: Broadway Books.

Harvey, Andrew. (2002). *The Sun at Midnight: A Memoir of the Dark Night.* New York NY: Jeremy Tarcher/Putnam

Holy Bible, New Oxford Annotated with the Apocrypha. (1973). Revised Standard Version. New York: Oxford University Press.

Holy Bible, New Stanford Alphabetical Indexed. (1951) Authorized King James Version. School and Library Reference Edition. Chicago: John A. Hertel Co.

Houston, Jean. (1987). *The Search for the Beloved: Journeys in Mythology and Sacred Psychology.* New York: Tarcher/Putnam.

Johnson, Robert. (1983). *We: Understanding the Psychology of Romantic Love.* New York: HarperCollins.

Johnson, Robert. (1993). *Owning Your Own Shadow: Understanding the Dark Side of the Psyche.* New York: Harper Collins.

Jung, Carl G, Aniela Jaffe, Clara Winston, and Richard Winston. (1989) *Memories, Dreams, Reflections.* New York: Vintage Books.

Kornfield, Jack. (2000). *After the Ecstasy, the Laundry: How the Heart Grows Wise on the Spiritual Path.* New York: Bantam.

Larson, Jeanne and Madge Micheels-Cyrus. (1986). *Seeds of Peace: A Catalogue of Quotations.* Gabriola Island, British Columbia, Canada: New Society Publishing.

Levoy, Gregg. (1997). *Callings: Finding and Following an Authentic Life.* New York: Three Rivers Press.

Matt, Daniel C. (1996). *The Essential Kabbalah: The Heart of Jewish Mysticism.* New York: HarperCollins.

McGaa, Edward, Eagle Man. (1990). *Mother Earth Spirituality: Native American Paths to Healing Ourselves and our World.* New York: HarperCollins.

Nerburn, Kent and Louise Mengelkoch. (1991). *Native American Wisdom (Classic Wisdom Collection)*. San Rafael CA: New World Library.

Pearson, Carol. (1991). *Awakening the Heroes Within: Twelve Archetypes to Help Us Find Ourselves and Transform Our World*. New York: HarperCollins.

Peck, M. Scott. (1987). *The Different Drum: Community Making and Peace*. New York: Touchstone.

Peck, M. Scott. (1998). *The Road Less Traveled: A New Psychology of Love, Traditional Values and Spiritual Growth*. New York: Touchstone.

Phillips, Bob (compiler). (1981) *The Last of the Good Clean Joke Books*. Eugene OR: Harvest House.

Sanford, John A. (1968, 1989). *Dreams: God's Forgotten Language*. San Francisco: Harper.

Shah, Indries. (1989). *The Exploits of the Incomparable Mullah Nasruddin*. London: Octagon Press.

Star, Jonathan and Sharam Shiva. (2006). *A Garden Beyond Paradise: Love Poems of Rumi*. Theone Press.

Swimme, Brian. (1994). *The Universe Story: From the Primordial Flaring Forth to the Ecozoic Era – A Celebration of the Unfolding of the Cosmos*. New York: HarperCollins.

Taylor, Jeremy, DMin (1983). *Dream Work: Techniques for Discovering the Creative Power in Dreams*. New Jersey: Paulist Press.

Taylor, Jeremy, DMin (1992). *Where People Fly and Water Runs Uphill: Using Dreams to Tap the Wisdom of the Unconscious.* New York: Warner Books.

Taylor, Jeremy, DMin (1998). *The Living Labyrinth: Exploring Universal Themes in the Myths, Dreams, and Symbolism of Waking Life.* New Jersey: Paulist Press.

Temple,Thurston, Leslie. (2000). *The Marriage of Spirit: Enlightened Living in Today's World.* Santa Fe, NM: CoreLight Publications.

Tolle, Eckhart. (2004). *The Power of Now: A Guide to Spiritual Enlightenment.* Novato, CA: New World Library.

Underhill, Evelyn. (1999). *Mysticism.* Oxford: Oneworld Publications.

Walters, Dorothy. (2002). *Unmasking the Rose: A Record of a Kundalini Initiation.* Charlottesville, VA: Hampton Roads.

Zukav, Gary. (1999). *Seat of the Soul.* New York: Simon and Schuster.

Zukav, Gary. (2000). *Soul Stories.* New York: Fireside.

Contact Information

For more information, and to order additional copies, please visit:

www.theunorthodoxlife.net